Doubt is a pain too lonely to know
that faith is his twin brother.

Khalil Gibran

God'shadow
Daniel de Sevén

BALM AND BLADE
PUBLISHING

First Edition, 2010
Layout and Design by Daniel de Sevén
Font: Helvetica Neue.

All rights reserved. No part of this book may be reproduced or transmitted in any form or by any means, electronic or mechanical, including photocopying and recording, or by any information storage and retrieval system, without permission in writing from the publisher.

God'shadow. Copyright © 2010 by Daniel de Sevén
ISBN: 978-0-9841386-3-0

Published by Balm and Blade Publishing
1475 Hollow Road
Birchrunville, PA 19421

www.balmandblade.com

All scripture quotations, unless otherwise indicated, are taken from the Holy Bible, Today's New International Version®. TNIV®. Copyright © 2001, 2005 by Biblica, Inc.™ Used by permission of Zondervan. All rights reserved worldwide.

www.zondervan.com

To JL,
    thank you for picking strawberries with me
    and for the many smiles you gave.
    may you continue to doubt your certainties.

Contents

a word...   iii

I. I Doubt

one.**The(o)sis**	1
two.**So Loved**	2
three.**I Doubt...**	5
four.**Questions**	9
five.**Blind Cartograpers**	11
six.**E8**	13
seven.**Bleeds**	14
eight.**Meaning i**	15
nine.**Refracted Factions**	16
ten.**Certain Uncertainty**	17
eleven.**Chariots of Fire**	19
twelve.**Conviction**	21
thirteen.**Doubt Like Rain**	22
fourteen.**Ex Nihilo**	23
fifteen.**Seeds**	25
sixteen.**Smile**	26
seventeen.**Ultima Thule**	28
eighteen.**Unconditional**	30
nineteen.**Pigeon Apocalypse**	31
twenty.**Soon***	35

II. Therefore I Think

twentyone.**Therefore I Think**	42
twentytwo.**Cyrene**	47
twentythree.**Promises, Promises**	49
twentyfour.**Meaning ii**	51
twentyfive.**When Angels Attack**	52
twentysix.**Woodstock**	55
twentyseven.**Expiration Date**	52
twentyeight.**Dreams**	59
twentynine.**Ba'al**	63
thirty.**Wept**	64
thirtyone.**Vivisection at the Intersection**	65
thirtytwo.**Existence Precedes Essence**	68
thirtythree.**Nietzsche Judged**	69
thirtyfour.**Two Worlds**	70
thirtyfive.**Thief**	71
thirtysix.**Ready (Or Not)**	73

III. Therefore I AM.

thirtyseven.**Disguised**	80
thirtyeight.**Therefore I AM**	83
thirtynine.**Ravine**	86
forty.**Jealousy**	87
fortyone.**Dirge**	89
fortytwo.**Snakes**	90
fortythree.**DH905569**	92
fortyfour.**She Is**	93
fortyfive.**Empty**	95
fortysix.**Home**	98
fortyseven.**Romance of the Divine**	102
fortytwo.**Fifteen Years**	104
fortyeight.**Three Movements**	107

fortynine.**Vicar**	109
fifty.**Brave**	112
fiftyone.**Catching Carmen**	113
fiftytwo.**Thank You, Jane Austen**	116
fiftythree.**In the Beginning Was the End**	120
Epilogue: **Descartes**	123
Index of the Scriptures	126
Eulogies	130

a word…

I find it very difficult to explain what's going on here. What kind of book is this, anyway? No scholarly footnotes, no central argument to support, and a boat load of ambiguous pronouns. I even made up a word or two.

Needless to say, I had a hard time pitching this project to the few who knew about it. "What's it about?" a barber asked once. "It's about…um…life and faith and stuff," I replied. Real helpful. I was a little more detailed when a waitress at Cracker Barrel caught me editing over breakfast. This time, I explained it as a book grappling with the polar existence of our spiritual natures. We're constantly torn between moral ideals and a concept of reality that is completely at odds with our senses. I think she was expecting me to describe a teen romance or a fantasy novel because her smile sank the moment it began to not sound like *Twilight*.

This book is roughly chiseled. Some of it is devotional, some is heretical, and some of it is abstract and almost mystical. Most of it will tempt you to doubt while some will push for you to believe. I don't say this to discourage you, but to outfit you for the challenge you face. I don't apologize for the fact that parts of it are controversial and even wrong. When you swing your mental hammer at it, I am fully aware that you will either break it or it will break you. That is the nature of it. I know that there might be some who will feel their faith weaken because of some of these questions raised. That's okay.

The goal is engagement. Even if you tear this book to shreds, I will be happy. So often we don't read critically enough, interacting with the author as he leads us on. I think we expect books to simply tell us what to think and are suspicious when the author is evasive or vague. We think things like: "What does the author have to hide? Why can't he just come right out and say it?" Plus, we are all caught up in this culture of busyness, moving too fast to think (how often do we abbreviate the word "you" as "u" in order to save two letters?). This is why I think most people don't like poetry in this age. And while this is by no means poetry, prose alike suffers from this uneasiness about thinking. This is, then, an effort to raise expectations and compel people to think about what they read. The fact that we have so much to do—so much to read—these days isn't an excuse not to be critical, but a powerful reason why we need to read things more carefully.

I've done my best to avoid giving you the straight out answers, even when I think I know what they are. This means that I don't agree with everything I wrote. I know that seems like a wicked cop out, but it is true. In this case it's not so much about what I think or believe but about what you think about what you believe. I feel that our Christian faith is better off with us having wrestled with these topics. You may find things you've never thought about or even things you are violently opinionated about. Just the same, take another look. Challenge yourself so that the answers you come up with are yours and no one else's. Even if you and I dis-

agree in the end, at least they're your answers.
So plunge forward and dare to doubt yourself.

And that is just the beginning...

    Daniel de Sevén
    December, 2009
    St. Louis, Missouri

Section I
I Doubt

one || the(o)sis

God is Love.

two || so loved

After all, Christians are so fond of reminding everyone that since the world is in such a horrible state of affairs Jesus is the only answer. Jesus said he'd wipe away every tear. Jesus said that whatever you give up in this life it will be given back to you with interest. Jesus said that he can raise the dead. Jesus said that he was a king. So it's pretty reasonable to expect that following Jesus covers everything.

But what bugs me is that things aren't covered. I just received a magazine from my church and inside was this article about a girl who goes to the same school as I do. She was going to visit her boyfriend in North Carolina when her car hit a wet spot and slid in front of an oncoming truck. She died instantly. She was 20.

Her aunt, Darlene, comforted her mother. But it was only a few years later when Darlene's own 16 year-old daughter, Julia, was diagnosed with a rare form of cancer. She died just a few days after graduation.

I wrestle with this. I can't get my mind around it. God, why didn't you save them?

Why wouldn't Jesus, who calls us both friends and family, help us? Why wouldn't he raise everyone from the dead? Why wouldn't he cure our diseases? It seems to me that when it comes to the weighty, transcendent moments in life, allegiances are moot. If you have the power to heal someone, you should, regardless of what "side" they're on.

But he didn't do these sort of things for his followers. Preachers get worked up on all the miracles Jesus did: he healed the blind, the paralyzed, the lepers, the infirm, the deformed, and the diseased. That's big news! But consider all the people Jesus didn't heal. Think of all the people he walked by. Think of all the people who needed him.

One Spring day, Jesus visited the pool of Bethesda. All around him was a writhing morass of sick people. Local legend had it that at a certain time each day an angel would come down and stir the waters would the tip of his finger. Then it was a mad frenzy to be the first in the pool, because the first one to jump in was healed. Those who finished second had a bitter crawl back to their nest of rags and straw.

Then came Jesus. He saw a guy next to him and asked the strangest question: "Would you like to get well?" This is the kind of question I end up asking whenever I go to visit someone in a hospital. I'm hopelessly awkward around sick people, and always end up asking things like "So, how are you feeling?" What do I expect them to say?

Jesus isn't awkward around sick people because he can actually heal them. But still, it's kind of awkward.

Jesus: "Do you want to get better?"

Man: "Yes, but I can't get to the pool fast enough."

Jesus: "So stand up, pick up your stuff, and go."

I'd probably be thinking, "Oh, like I never thought of that before!" But the man had faith, not sarcasm, and ended up being healed. End of story.

But what about all the other people there? Didn't they want to be healed? Did they really not have faith? It seems like an immense injustice: to have the power over death and exercise it so selectively. What are Jesus' criteria for choosing who to heal? How does he decide who to save from cancer and who to let go? Those two girls believed him. And don't tell me it's a bad world and stuff happens...blah blah. If you loved someone, if you really loved them, there is no way you'd stand by and let them die. She never saw the car coming, but God did.

three || I doubt

It all began with a question. Questions are always hard. To ask a question means you have to admit your own ignorance or inability. Every question is a tiny check against your pride. Some questions require great courage. Some questions dig away at the foundation of everything you've built.

"How can God ever satisfy our ability to doubt?"

I know that seems like a really esoteric question, but its implications are enormous.

Have you ever known someone who was utterly stubborn when confronted with irrefutable proof? You can put all the pieces of the puzzle together, but if you're missing just one they'll refuse to see the whole picture. I used to think I was being so philosophically dangerous by declaring that I wasn't sure I could prove I even existed. People will always believe what they want to believe.

Think of how this discussion would have gone with Plato, who was among those ancient Greeks who didn't think the world was really real:

Plato: "This table is just a shadow of the real table somewhere in the universe."

Me: "It looks like a pretty solid table to me. Look, I can jump on it."

Plato: "That's just an illusion of sorts."

Me: "But I can *jump* on it!"

Plato: "Can you?"

Me: "Watch…me…I…am…jumping!"

Plato: "I can see that, but you aren't jumping on a table."

Me: "Then what do you call this wooden thing under my feet?"

Plato: "A shadow."

Me: "You are buying me lunch."

God can't force us to believe. Even when God's voice thundered down from the shrouded peaks of Sinai and the people trembled in absolute terror, they managed to make a golden calf just days later. Maybe you didn't get that: *In the very presence of God, when there was irrefutable physical, empirical evidence right in front of their faces, they still managed to doubt whether he really was the real thing.* Human beings have an amazing capacity for doubt.

The really amazing thing is how many people never believed in Jesus when he was on this earth. Everything he said was perfect. Every act and thought was in love. He couldn't have done one thing any better, and yet the vast multitude of people he encountered didn't believe in him. God himself was talking with them face to face and it wasn't enough.

So what will prevent some knucklehead from getting to heaven and ten thousand years later refusing to believe? It's completely hypothetical, I know, but it's possible. After all, both doubt and sin originated in heaven.

We often assume that heaven is this place of perpetual bliss where nothing can ever fail and angels resemble Precious Moments figurines. It's the immediate solution to all our problems. Sometimes Christians have this idealized happy-state-of-mind outlook on heaven. We see it simply as the solution or the reward.

But heaven is a real place. While the Scriptures don't tell us everything that will happen when life is renewed, we are given strange glimpses of our life there. John writes that he saw the Tree of Life, whose "leaves are for the healing of the nations." This suggests that heaven will be a place of growth and healing, too. We may have battle scars and emotional problems to work through. God can't snap his fingers and make everything magically better. It takes time, even in eternity.

We may very well carry our doubts into heaven and we'll certainly carry our capacity to doubt there. Many of us have deep doubts, hidden wounds that cut us sharply.

Have you ever felt so sure that God wanted you to do something and it was a total disaster?

Have you ever prayed hard (but futilely) as a rare disease took such a gifted young person away?

Have you ever asked but not received?

Have you ever wondered whether we made this whole thing up? That we just want God to be there because we're scared of life?

Have you ever had serious doubts about the goodness of God?

It's okay to think about these things. God isn't offended that you have doubts. After all, doubts can make your faith stronger.

four || questions

You can't tell me that my questions aren't valid. Why do you always make me feel like asking is the same as doubting? It seems to me that your answers are afraid of my questions. Why? If God loves us, doesn't he want us to know? If he didn't make us as robots but gave us free will—as you're so fond of saying—then doesn't he mind us exercising freedom of inquiry?

Job was an awesome Christian. He never did anything wrong, and when God allowed the devil to torment him didn't he say: "I cry out to you, God, but you do not answer....You turn on me ruthlessly; with the might of your hand you attack me"? Job said God had become ruthless with him. I'm not saying he was right or he was wrong; the fact remains that someone who was a lot closer to God than I am dared to question and accuse God.

The prophet Jeremiah also had questions. Early on in his journey he told God: "You are always righteous, Lord, when I bring a case before you. Yet I would speak with you about your justice: Why does the way of the wicked prosper? Why do all the faithless live at ease?" And just to drive the point home, Jeremiah adds: "You have planted them, and they have taken root."

Or let's talk about Solomon, who some have said was the wisest man to ever live. Do you know what he learned about life? "Surely the fate of human beings is like that of the animals; the same fate awaits them both: As one dies, so dies the other. All have the same breath; humans have no advantage over animals. Everything is meaningless."

I'm in good company.

Why are we so afraid of questions? Are we afraid that everything will unravel? What does that say about your view of God? What does it say about mine?

five || the blind cartographers

But then you came. You insisted on coming. First you gave us the stars, and then the moon, and then completed your destruction of our world with the sun. We could see. We could see and we hated you for it. Some insisted on claiming they were still blind, but the honest ones amongst us knew we could never go back. A line had been crossed.

We were content. We were the blind cartographers. In our world of woven shadows we shared the suffering of sin (though we didn't know its name).

How can I help but conclude that this doubt is from God? that all doubt is from God?

Our world took a vastly different shape. Whereas in blindness our clumsiness was forgiven, now we had to be careful where we stepped. Trees and mountains appeared, whose grim outline was our only previous acquaintance. We learned we could climb them and fall from them.

I just want to know why. Why did you put this doubt in me? Why did you give me this heavy burden of sight? Now I am responsible for what I see.

There were no shadows in the blind darkness. But now the sun—your light—casts such long shadows in our hearts we know not what to do but commit the darkness to you. Now hiding in the shadows isn't a way to live. These doubts are from you. I never had them before. At one point I took everything by faith. Now I can see and it is a struggle. But I'll never forget that it was you who made me to see.

The shadow is in my heart. But it is your shadow.

six || E8

One time I went to the funeral of a truly evil person. He was the guy who always came to church with something to confess, and then went out and did things that were even worse. But the people gave him such flowery eulogies—people from the very neighborhood where he did these things.

Because God takes so long to punish evil people, they think they can get away with murder.

But even though bad people do bad things, I still think that it's better that people follow God. Someday their luck will run out, and justice will catch up with them. They don't respect God, so every day is just a shadow of what awaits...

seven || bleeds

We need a Christianity that bleeds. Look at that gold cross around her neck. Look at how it glimmers in that bright sunlight. It looks great; it matches her earrings well.

They left it in the ground, you know. But we took it. We wiped it off, sanded it down, and put it in a museum. They shrunk away from it in fear while we shrugged it off. It was to be the symbol of a new era, but in reality it describes neither the dead Savior nor the living one, but one that never was. No one ever died on a golden cross.

It was an instrument of death and on it He bled love until our oceans became red; until the whole world drank up their guilt. But we have tamed his love and we have filtered our water.

Someone once asked me why Christianity is such a bloody religion. They scoffed that people who have followed Christ have had the blood of innocents on their hands. I scoffed too, knowing that those sins happened precisely because they *didn't* have the blood of Innocence on their hands.

We have a Christianity that bleeds.

eight || meaning i

Tell that to Jean-Paul Sartre, who said that "life has no meaning the moment you lose the illusion of being eternal." Maybe that's what this Christian thing is: an unwillingness to let go. Maybe it's arrogance, an old-style power grab in penitent garb. Maybe it's an illusion. Maybe I can't cope with the idea that there's nothing out there. I'm clinging to the edge of the branch, refusing to look down because I'm afraid of how high I've climbed up the tree. What if I fall?

What if there's nothing below? What if there's nothing *above*?

nine || refracted factions

"Everyone agrees: red is better than orange. Red is bold, visceral, and romantic. It is the color that daringly dashes in and the one left bleeding when everyone else has left. It is the color of sin...and redemption. Orange is so...vitamin C. If you were to put red and orange next to each other, orange would blush in embarrassment and become red."

Dear saints, don't you see? Only the blind argue over color, for one who sees sees that all color is one—a single beam, fragmented, explained, and refracted in our lives. There is only one truth, and it was broken for us so we could apprehend it. True Light is too pure for our eyes. We can only see the hues. Why then do we argue over which aspect of Truth is the greatest? Why do you cherish yellow and spurn violet?

Do you not seek the True White robes of heaven? And what is that White, if it is not the character of a person who reflects all the hues?

ten || certain uncertainty

Have you ever thought about how much we want it to be true? It's almost as if we need it to be true. We all have this deep-seated insecurity for security in the deepest part of our hearts. We all want certainty.

But the only thing certain is uncertainty.

We have quizzes and awards for people who know things. We reward certainty because certainty seems like conviction. And in a world of doubts and, worse yet, doubters, anyone with any certainty (even pretended) is a leader.

Take a man with bad eyesight visiting a village market in northern Africa. He hears the familiar notes of a charmer's flute and notices a long, slender thing rising from a basket. "Come near," another man says, encouraging him. But what is the thing? Is it a rope? Is it a snake? Is it something else? It is impossible to tell.

None of us really know much for certain. We don't know how we got here. Sure, some will say we can demonstrate this with microscopes and telescopes, but how do we really know they're not as blind as the man in the village? We have to assume that our senses are absolute—that we can derive truth from what we can see. And yet we wouldn't know if we had bad eyesight or not. What would we compare ourselves to?

This is all increasingly obvious in an age of specialized knowledge. Whereas in the past you might have been able to get a broad degree in something and move on, now the explosion of knowledge has created a need for increased specialization. The result is that we "know" more and more about a subject while simultaneously knowing less and less. You can spend your whole life studying the mating habits of a certain monkey and know nothing at all about farming or fashion or literature.

This means that, as time goes on, we will need each other more just to survive. There are too many gaps in our knowledge of the world. We cannot possibly know everything. So what happens when you begin to doubt what little you do know? Where does that leave you?

Try it. Think of everything you take for granted as stable and secure. Pick everything apart. Ask questions you've been afraid to ask: What if there are times she doesn't love you? What if he doesn't respect you? What if we're not alone in the galaxy? What if your life has been wasted? What if you were wrong…?

We need security. And we can turn to science as much as we can turn to God for it. We have to put our faith somewhere. No one can be a pure doubter; you have to accept something as true and valuable if you want to live.

But first we must be unafraid to ask the questions. We must be unafraid of uncertainty.

eleven || chariots of fire

"Hullo, Turtle." Rabbit caught up to his old friend. "It's a beautiful day out, isn't it?" Rabbit hopped along next to him a little quicker than was necessary.

Turtle said nothing.

"I thought we should talk, you know, about the race." And since Rabbit knew he was faster, there wasn't much Turtle could do but listen.

"I know that you won—I admit that—and that everyone is excited that the slow turtle beat the fast rabbit. Everyone loves the underdog and all. But you do realize that had I ran straight for the finish line I would have won, right? Now I don't want to seem the sore loser, but I thought you ought to know that 'slow and steady wins the race' is a joke. Fast wins the race. Fast always wins the race. I am just afraid you're going to get a hero complex over this. They may praise you now, but in the next race they'll put their money on me."

Turtle said nothing.

"Don't feel discouraged, Turtle. It's not your fault that you are slow. You were made that way and I was made fast. People don't mount turtles into battle, they ride horses. People don't breed turtles for shows. People can watch cheetahs and eagles for a lot longer than they can watch turtles. Nature seems to prefer us over you. But don't become bitter. I don't want to see you hiding in your shell and crying about this. Accept fate and go on living. I know there are some who say that in the end the last will be first and all, but that's really stuff invented by the losers of races to make themselves feel better. Don't buy into it. It's victim-thinking. Please rise above this."

Rabbit lingered a few more minutes before smiling to himself and hopping away, satisfied at imparting another of life's little pearls.

Turtle said nothing, and instead began to walk a little slower.

twelve || conviction

You tie my hands and tell me to shovel twice as fast. I was happy volunteering, but this is something different. God, I beg of you: don't make me do this. Don't make me go down this road. You set me to work digging my own grave. You've promised new life and a fresh start, but, God, how hard it is to take the first breath!

thirteen || doubt like rain

We all love the sunny days. We plan our days around the certainty of sunlight—volleyball, getting a tan, going to the beach. And when it rains, our plans change. It's not as fun when it rains. We can't tell—even with a college degree—when it will rain. Rain is like doubt. It pools and eddies and streams and rushes by recklessly.

But all creation needs the rain. And we shouldn't forget that the sun starves the earth and burns the skin. Too much certainty makes you thirst for doubt, for unorthodoxy, because we know that life is less certain. Theology must always agree with life. When it doesn't fit, we look for something else. We cannot be too certain of these things, lest we dry up and die. We need water. Doubt like rain.

fourteen || ex nihilo

Whether you believe in God or not, it doesn't matter. Either way, it all began with nothing. Nothing of any consequence. This ragged clod of dirt is here. We are here. Whether of ooze or dirt; whether planned or accidental, we are here. Either way, it all began with nothing and nothing is the foundation for something.

How can we live this way?

I think I can agree with Nietzsche, who said that "he who has a 'why' to live can bear with almost any 'how.'" I need that "why." But does it even exist outside of the "how" we were created with? Does it really make any difference whether some eternal being stooped down to carve me out of this dysfunctional rock or whether I emerged from some cosmic spit? Either way, I am tied to this place. I am part of the problem.

We owe it to ourselves not just to demand the answer but to find it. Our increasing isolation as meaningless anomalies leads our collective sub-consciousness into despair. Every day science uncovers more and more reasons for why things previously wrapped in a shadow of awe are now mundane and predictable. What was sacred—human life, human sex, human children—is easier and easier to explain away. Without that sacredness, what is so special about us? How are we any different from animals, except that we seem half-blessed and twice-cursed by comparison? Show me a squirrel with a broken marriage or an eagle with a mortgage.

How can we live this way?

The structure of our lives—our pretended confidence in our careers, our families, and our countries—rests on a foundation of nothingness. We teeter and totter on the brink of an infinite chasm and when someone falls in we weep and wail as if some great tragedy has happened. What did you think was going to happen? Where did you think all of this was going? Did they… mean something to you? Why?

Our atmosphere insulates us. It protects us from what is the only important fact: we are alone. We are isolated and surrounded by dark, unforgiving blackness. We just hang here, ignorant of the harshest possible environment just outside our windows. At any moment we could be erased without remorse. There would be no one to remember us. This isn't depression; this is reality.

But we are here.

We are something.

There is something in this nothingness.

fifteen || seeds

"Couldn't he stop it if he wanted to?"

Carrot thought for a moment. With one finger he scratched his leafy green hair.

"I guess so."

Rabbit continued: "All I'm saying is that if the farmer really wanted rabbits to eat something other than carrots, he wouldn't have planted you. Or else he would have put me in a cage or given me an appetite for something else. So you understand then that I have no choice but to eat you? It's what the farmer wants."

"Still, it doesn't seem fair. I don't harm anyone."

"I know it isn't fair, but this is how it goes. This time I can do you a favor though and go eat another carrot if you'd like."

"Golly, that would be nice of you."

"Anytime."

sixteen || smile

I saw him smile. He couldn't have been more than 10. Life smiled back. He ran up and asked the lady for a piece of chocolate. She offered him one, but he frowned. I heard him tell her that he had a sister too and he wondered if it'd be OK to give her one too. But the lady didn't have another, so he took none. The lady was absolutely enchanted by such a noble young boy. He wasn't going to eat if his sister didn't get something also. He was raised well, we'd say, and he had lots to smile about.

But I saw some other little boys once who didn't smile. They were being kidnapped (but told they were being "set free"), given guns ("to save people"), and trained as soldiers ("freedom fighters") to destroy the government ("set the country free"). They weren't raised by men, but monsters. What did they have to smile about?

So I realized that it's a short fall from a smile to a frown. Some kids never have a fair chance. I wonder who I would be if an army invaded my city, or if there was a food shortage, or some plague ruined this glass house of order I take for granted. It really wouldn't take much to bring it all crashing down.

Who would I be in this other world? What would I be like when I'm really tested? If the flame of divine scrutiny were really put to me, how much would be dross and how much would be gold? If I had to literally fight to feed my family and friends, would I lose my lofty ideals about non-violence and loving one's neighbor? So how can I really blame those people who are put to the fire every day, while I sit here apathetically on my sofa basking in the warmth and glow of the same fire? Don't I realize that they are the logs I put in? Is it clear to everyone but me that we will tolerate genocide in Africa so long as it doesn't lead to us having to forfeit watching movies about genocide?

Why have I been cursed with this blessedness when I use it to further my own ignorance?

Am I really who I seem when I sit so far from the fire?

seventeen || ultima thule

Have you noticed it, too?

We never quite arrive. But we're always searching.

Look at all the stories in our lives—the movies, the books, our little experiences—and count how many are all about finding the unknown. Maybe it's a new life form or an undiscovered island. We're enchanted about new inventions and buzzing over the possibilities of change.

We're always pushing ourselves higher, farther, deeper…

But to where?

Who has stopped and asked the question, "Where are we going?"

The ancient Greeks searched for this place called *ultima thule*. It was that place just beyond reach, another horizon away. Some claimed to have been there, with one describing it as a placed made of something like Jello-O. Later on, people thought it was Iceland or Greenland. Some claimed it didn't exist at all.

But now the world is mapped. Satellites circle overhead, watching. GPS devices can tell you where every gas station and red rock is from here to Vietnam. Cell phones, with the exception of AT&T, can connect you with anyone almost anywhere. Google gives you every fact at your fingertips. We are getting it all figured out. What part of the globe remains out of our reach?

Yet the thrill of the unknown is not lost to us. National Geographic had a story not too long ago about the discovery of dozens and dozens of new species. The headline of the article said this "trove of new species" was found in a "lost world." Doesn't it sound exciting? It's a "lost world"—one that we lost amidst all of our "finding" out about things. The unspoken conclusion to this kind of news is: "I wonder what else we haven't discovered out there?"

That's the question we could be asking.

eighteen || unconditional

I enjoy being in the arms of another—someone who loves me for what they can get out of me, because I know I can give. For when I give, they give back— that's security.

You say you love me unconditionally and that you love me for who I am. I don't want you to love me for who I am, because I don't like who I am. Nor do I want you to love me unconditionally, because everything we do has reason and conditions. To love without reason is reckless and scary. I have no control over it; it's so strange. When I hang up on you or walk out in the middle of one of your speeches, it doesn't faze you. It's like you can love me without me. Nothing I do affects you. I don't like being powerless. I like conditions. Conditions mean I can do something to make you love me more.

But you say you can't love me more than you do. How is that possible? What did I do to deserve it? Why are you so unrelenting? It makes me nervous. I feel like I'm missing some great truth about life that makes you the way you are. Or maybe you're just crazy. Maybe I'm crazy, because even though I don't understand you, even though I keep going to people whose love I can influence and adjust, I keep coming home to you. This constant, unconditional love you have is what repulses me…and what makes me repent.

nineteen || the pigeon apocalypse

We're all going to die. How cheerful.

It could be exciting: nuclear holocaust, Meteor hurtling toward earth, Godzilla runs amok, flu vaccine turns everyone into zombies, etc. Or perhaps it might be less fantastic: global pandemic, the sun explodes, global warming, or the Yankees go a decade without going to the World Series.

So many movies, books, and T.V. shows come out every year trying to depict how it's all going to end. We've got every angle covered, so that some imaginative writer can step forward just before we are eaten by mutant pigeons and say, "Aha! I saw that one coming!" How comforting. What astounding foresight.

What's behind this strange preoccupation in our extinction, anyway? I doubt the dinosaurs amused themselves by scratching elaborate depictions of death-by-ice-age before they went extinct. But we find it entertaining; it makes for some interesting conversation at lunch: "Why did the Mayan calendar run out in 2012, anyway?"

Perhaps our fascination with the end is natural. We almost intuitively look for an end. We expect it. Every story has its happily-ever-after, every movie rolls the credits, every plant and animal dies, everyone has to say goodbye at some point. Why shouldn't humanity have to say goodbye at some point too? Everything is mortal, everything is corruptible, and everyone falls at least once.

Our very existence seems to demand an end, so why not imagine it to be with a bang rather than a whimper? Let an asteroid come and wipe us out. We'll be martyrs at the hand of the universe. It's certainly more poetic than killing each other in a war.

Perhaps our fascination with the end is our way of escaping the tedious tension of life. We're born to steal and not to share. But we do a lot of good things too. We're stuck between good and bad, always having to choose one or the other. Or we're confronted by insoluble questions like whether God exists or not. No one can go through life ignoring that one. We all have to choose something, and that something might have serious consequences.

We live our lives without perfect certainty about so many things. Who knows for sure whether there is an afterlife or not? Did I make the right choices? Will my kids appreciate me when I'm gone? What if I die in a car accident tonight? So many questions betray our basic uneasiness about life. We have no control. There are so very few things we can be confident about, and that breeds insecurity. If we're going to function at all, we have to block out a lot of these questions, ignore the blanks, and tell ourselves it's the right answer.

You wake up and find yourself out in the desert. You ask yourself which way will take you toward civilization but the cacti are all pointing in difference directions.

You can't wander around forever. At some point you have to pick the way that seems most promising and hope you're right in the end. If you stay at the starting point asking all the logical questions, you'll die where you started. We don't have all the answers. So we risk it. We have to if we want to lead any kind of normal life.

But deep inside we want to be released from the burden of living. We want to be freed from the tension of always having to pick a side, of being unsure about so many things. So we look to the end. It's not that we are morbid or suicidal. We just intuitively grasp that we can't live in this kind of paradox forever. We are frail, mortal beings with dreams of immortality. Deer don't dream of flying. Squirrels don't imagine what life would be like living forever. We alone have the capacity to dream but the inability to make all of our dreams come true. We're puzzles missing a piece and we can sense it. Maybe we somehow sense that there is some kind of cosmic controversy going on that we're forced to take sides on. So we simply look to the end.

Humanity has always felt the end was near. It isn't a recent development. Every so often we get into a frenzy of speculation and wonder at whether it will be soon. People in Europe thought the world was going to end around A.D. 1000. The Maya insist the world has ended and been recreated four times already. Some Christians thought Jesus would come back in 1844, 1917, and lots of other dates. And let's not forget the worry over Y2K. Every natural disaster or nuclear-backed bravado seems to reawaken the idea of the end in someone's mind.

Our history is littered with hundreds of examples of human beings anticipating the end. Every story needs an end, and we spend a lot of time thinking about ours. Some of the ideas that people have are totally crazy. The point isn't to get caught up in the "how" the end will happen, but to notice the consensus we've reached that it will happen. What if the anticipation is natural? What if it's logical that we should be so fascinated with the end?

It's not just a religious thing. It's a human thing.

twenty || soon*

As you're stirring your signature dish, tofu toupée, you get a call from your arriving guest: "Hey, I'm running a little late. I'll be there soon." That's not too abnormal. You imagine he or she is 10, 15, maybe 20 minutes behind. Just dial down the heat a little and keep it warm.

But what if your guest is 2,000 years late?

Anyone who reads the Bible can't help but become a little confused about Jesus' definition of "soon." Over and over, Jesus tells stories and makes statements about the fact that he's going to return after he ascends into heaven. Entire chapters like Matthew 24 and 25 deal with the end times and the signs that point to his coming. And in the book of Revelation, there are ten references in the first and last chapter about all of these things happening soon. You can't miss it:

> "Look, I am coming soon!"
> "Look, I am coming soon!"
> "Yes, I am coming soon."

Apparently astute at discerning Jesus' subtlety, John writes after the last assurance: "Amen. Come, Lord Jesus." These are the last words Jesus spoke in the Bible: he tells us three times that he's coming soon.

That's significant. Usually when something is said three times in the Bible it shows us that the thing is really certain and complete. Peter denied that he knew Jesus three times. As part of his redemption Jesus asked Peter three times if he loved him. We tell people things like, "Don't make me ask you twice!" because we feel if we have to repeat something then it implies that the listener didn't care enough to hear it the first time. But we also repeat things we expect people to remember. For the people of Jesus' day, it was a symbolic act. It wasn't that Jesus mistrusted Peter and kept asking him the same question until he was sure. The repeated question was meant as an opportunity for Peter to really affirm his love for Jesus, akin to showing the completeness of his resolve. So when Jesus tells us three times in Revelation that he is coming soon, it's meant to inspire confidence in what he says.

But, if you haven't noticed, that was a long time ago.

Peter tries to comfort us in his second letter by reminding us that for God time is pretty fluid. For God, a thousand years can pass in an hour or vice versa. So "soon" for him could be ten thousand years in our time. But that totally sounds like a cop out. As if some day God will look at his watch and suddenly remember, "Oh, I totally forgot that time moves much slower down there. I better hurry, and apologize for being late."

But I don't think Peter was implying we should cut God some slack because, hey, we all make mistakes. Jesus made the promise in our time zone and with us in mind. He tells us he is coming soon to give us hope. It would kind of defeat the purpose if he used an unfamiliar definition of the word "soon."

Peter is actually alluding to one of the Psalms that Moses wrote, which tells us that "a thousand years in your sight are like a day that has just gone by." In other words, God is wholly unbound by our conception of time. Moses wants us to see how powerful God is. When we look back a thousand years ago to the time around 1000 A.D., it might as well be a gazillion years ago. So much has changed since then. And, beyond that, we really cannot appreciate a number so big. We can't visualize a thousand of anything. But for God a thousand is a very small number.

Peter just wants us to keep things in perspective. I know I grumble when it takes longer than 3.5 seconds for my e-mail to load. When it hits the twenty-second mark, I crawl over to the modem to see if maybe the Internet stopped working. At thirty seconds, people die. The point is, I think Peter is making an argument against the inevitable erosion of faith that happens the longer someone is asked to believe. It's pretty easy to hold on in faith when you're asked to wait five minutes. But when you're asked to hold on five hours or five days or five years or five hundred years it gets harder. You start to wonder whether God just forgot his promise or whether he lied. Peter's point is that we shouldn't lose faith because for God, it's as if he made the promise yesterday. He hasn't forgotten with the passing of time and neither should we.

Once Jesus was telling a story of a widow. Now, widows in those days were completely dependent on friends and family to help them. But this widow had no one to help her. It wasn't long before people began preying on her, swooping in on their helpless victim. The woman, naturally, ran to the local judge and presented her case in the hopes that he'd protect her. But the judge ignored the case. There were too many other things to do. Yet the woman was persistent. She kept pestering the judge until one day he was so fed up that he agreed to help her because, the Bible tells us, he feared that the woman had grown so persistent that she might beat him up. But then Jesus makes a strange point. He says, if an apathetic judge could eventually be persuaded to give a person justice how much more would the Father give justice to those he loves? "Will he keep putting them off?" Jesus asks. To put it another way: will God keep delaying, frustrating our hopes?

The implied answer is "no." He will come! "When the Son of Man comes," he asks, "will he find faith on the earth?" Will there be anyone left holding on who will still have faith in my coming? In other words, he wants to know if you and I are going to be like that widow, praying and pleading for God to come until he finally does. After all, Luke tells us the parable was given so "that they should always pray and not give up."

In the Book of Revelation, we're given a similar picture. When Jesus opens the fifth seal we see a picture of people who had been killed for Jesus' sake calling out and asking how long they are supposed to wait before Jesus comes and gives them justice. The answer comes back that they were all to wait "a little longer."

You see, Jesus isn't ignorant of the terrible predicament this delay has put us in. He knows that it is awfully awkward to preach the reality that Jesus is coming soon some 2,000 years after the promise was given. He told us it was going to be soon, but that we ought to expect a delay.

That inspires me. I mean, he warned us that he'd be later than we think. In other places he tells us that he was coming like a thief in the night or that his coming will be like lightening. We can't anticipate his arrival with any exactitude. In Matthew 25 he tells three stories, two of which feature a delay of the hero in arriving to save the day. Jesus knew he'd be later than we expect, and even told us that so we wouldn't lose hope long before we had any.

This isn't the first time a coming has seemed delayed. God deals with large numbers. Who could have convinced Adam and Eve that it would taken 4,000 years for the savior they were promised to come? Jude tells us that Enoch, the seventh generation from Adam, preached that God was coming soon to judge the world. And that was when the world was at the beginning of all of this! Noah preached for 120 years that a flood was coming, and in the end God shut him in the ark and nothing happened. The flood was delayed an extra seven days as Noah's faith was really put to the test. On and on it goes throughout history. There are many examples of God arriving later than anticipated, but always on time. Why should it be of any special worry to us?

The really interesting thing that Jesus does when he tells the story about the widow is that he links his coming with his justice. When we might be asked to give a list of the reasons why Jesus is coming back, we usually focus on the benefits it gives us. We remind people that there will be no more war, that pain will end, and that we'll be restored to the companionship of loved ones. But Jesus lets us know that his coming isn't a one-sided event. People are crying out to him for help because he has claimed to be our Savior. He has an obligation then to answer those prayers. He must come back to deal with them and in a timely manner. He can't put it off forever. He has staked his reputation on it. He didn't come all this way to die on a cross and then abandon us. The cross itself demands that he has to come back again. It's immensely comforting to realize that not only does he want to come back but he has to as well. He can't continue to be who he says he is if he doesn't. This promise, if unfulfilled, cancels out every other promise he made. God has risked himself on this promise to finish what he started. And it will be…

…Soon*

Section II
Therefore I Think

twenty-one || therefore I think

The Syrian king was perplexed. He had been sending bands of soldiers into Israel's lands to plunder what they could before slipping back across the border. But the return on his investment was dwindling each time. "What gives?" he wondered. The Israelites used to wander like lemmings right into his ambushes. Suddenly they were as cunning as foxes and avoided every trap.

"There's a traitor that's giving away our plans," the king proclaimed to his army officers.

"Now who is it?" The king wasn't one to beat around the bush.

"It's that Israelite prophet, Elisha, who is telling their king where we're going to attack," the Joint Chiefs replied.

To which the Syrian king said, "You knew this? And you were planning on telling me this when...?" It wasn't too long before somebody in that room was headed to Israel with a lot more than a raiding party.

I would have been the guy to raise my hand.

Syrian King: "Yes, Daniel?"

Me: "I was wondering if your awesomeness has considered the possibility that since Elisha knows of our raids in advance, he might know of this attack headed towards him in advance, also?"

Syrian King: "Yeah, you ask too many questions, kid."

Me: "Furthermore, has anyone here given thought to exactly how this man knows so much? If it is true that his god is telling him all of our plans, then maybe attacking him is a bad idea. And if it is a traitor among your soldiers, then why aren't we trying to find him?"

Syrian King: "That's why I am attacking at night. If he does receive a vision at night, by the time he wakes up the city will be surrounded. If it is a traitor in my camp, Elisha will prove it one way or the other. Clever, huh?"

Elisha's servant got the message. He stared over the walls of the city and saw the Syrian army grinning back. It was like every member in his extended family suddenly showed up at his doorstep. "Surprise!" It wasn't too hard to figure out why they were there.

"Elisha," his servant cried, "What are we going to do? There are," the servant counted the Syrians one-by-one, "a lot of them."

"Lord," Elisha sighed, "open his eyes." The Scriptures tell us that the servant saw thousands upon thousands of angels in God's army surrounding the army that was surrounding the city.

Elisha's prayer implies that his servant's problem wasn't cowardice but blindness. He literally didn't see any way out of the situation. So he doubted and despaired. Who could really blame him? Most of us are where the servant is, on the fault line of the visible and invisible, the heavenly and earthly. Most of the doubts we have about God exist because we are in this horrible tension between the life of unseen eternity and the life of the physical, here-and-now. We are constantly forced to contend with the temporary nature of what we experience, when the things we experience tell us they'll last forever. Every great feat of man, along with every massive mountain, suggests permanence and optimism.

Christ wants us to know that what we see down here isn't what's really real. It's not what we should plan for or count on in the long term. But that kind of thinking is counter-intuitive. It goes against the grain. God doesn't blame us for having doubts, for having difficulty trying to live in an unseen reality. The friction along that fault line is only natural.

But the reality is that heaven isn't some distant place. The armies of God are here and now, fighting an unseen battle that rages sleeplessly on our streets and in our skies. Every temptation we face is a skirmish involving untold numbers of allied and enemy soldiers. But we are largely oblivious. The idea that a pitiful earthly army like the one the Syrians fielded provoked a reaction from God's army is really incredible. It shows us that God takes the protection of his people seriously. To be sure, God didn't need a whole company of angels to take the field against the Syrians. But there were likely darker powers at work, spurring the Syrians on to fight a proxy war against Elisha and God's faithful mortals. It was to them that the armies of heaven responded. So don't think that God just looks down from on high and arbitrarily intervenes. We need to understand God's actions in the larger context of a universal war and not succumb to the temptation to think that our reality is the only one that matters. In truth, we are blind.

So it strikes me as a little strange when people suggest that Christians aren't reasonable people, as if faith is based on whims and emotions. Everybody uses reason as the basis for their beliefs. The only difference is the starting point. If you don't think that God exists, then it is indeed natural to see religion as a self-delusion, as mere wish fulfillment, or as a great, parasitical evil. That makes sense. But if you believe God is real and revealed, and that we are blind to the larger universe, then it makes perfect sense for believers to live as if they will never die, while talking of the need to die daily. It's perfectly reasonable if that is your starting point.

The question is always of your first principle,

that core idea like the wheat that remains after the chaff has been winnowed. For me, it's the idea that I am wrong somehow. I aim high but fall short more often than not. Yet I feel I am more than the sum of my parts. I feel the inner tension between what I want to do and what I actually do. So when I read similar words in Paul, I knew I wasn't the only one. The Bible calls it "sinfulness." And so I chose this path because I felt it was the only answer that adequately fit the problem of me.

What is your starting point? After you doubt everything, what remains?

Elisha's servant came to see the reality that his master knew. But he had to pass through doubt before he could find certainty. He had to question. He had to acknowledge his blindness before he could see. Try to see things from Elisha's perspective. Don't throw up your hands and judge God the moment you can't see how things will work out. Sometimes it is impossible to think of one way God can extricate himself from the tomb he buried himself in within your heart. But you will see that God is full of all sorts of surprises. At any time he may be invisibly surrounding the enemies that surround you. I am not saying all your questions will be answered immediately but try and look beyond your physical circumstances for a while. Give God the benefit of your doubts. Give God your doubts.

twenty-two || cyrene

We spend $60,000 and six weeks to tell a dozen people that Jesus is coming soon. Yet so many people feel Jesus has already come and walked on by them—some poor, some homeless, some sick, some just out of luck. What does a second coming mean to those who never experienced the first one? How can they be excited that he will soon return to judge the world when they missed the fact that he first came to heal the sick?

I don't really blame them. We mean well, but well enough to change? We tell them what's true—and who can argue with that?—but who teaches them why the truth matters? How many homeless will respond to a brochure that arrives at an address they don't have? Bibles don't keep people warm at night.

Blame it on the preacher if you want. After all, it was his fiery sermon that put that fire within you. "Get out and 'win' souls. If you love Jesus you will tell others." Guilt-trip evangelism just makes more people guilty.

We don't need this kind of Christianity. It only offers its cross to others.

Let's go to the neighborhoods; let's ask them if they know of our church on the corner. Ask them what they know about it. Ask them if there are good people there. Ask them if lives have been changed there. Ask them if their streets are safer because of it, if their children are happier. Ask them if the church means anything to them. Stop mailing invitations. Stop selling books. Stop valuing people only for their capacity to hear your message. Stop to listen. Come empty-handed.

twenty-three || promises, promises…

That's life. Ironic, even. We pledge our undying love, but it's we who die. Only immortals can promise eternity to each other. But we have a tendency to forget ourselves, to get caught up in the divine current that passes through us and for a moment—just a brief moment—we have a flash of immortality. We promise the sun and the moon as if they're ours to give.

Promises. Whether love is divine or chemical, it's we who are the weakest link in the equation. We make commitments to people without really knowing them. We want to believe that people are honest and sincere. Life doesn't work if we don't take a chance and love before it's safe to love. The world orbits around this kind of faith.

"This is what the Lord says," Isaiah tells us, "Do not fear, for I have redeemed you; I have summoned you by name; you are mine….Since you are precious and honored in my sight, and because I love you, I will give nations in exchange for you."

God, too, takes a chance. But his promises are different. Unlike us, he knows what he's getting into. He knows me better than I know myself, and yet he still claims to love me? Would he still give up entire nations just for me? I just want to laugh at such audacious naivety! Maybe God is a blind optimist like the rest of us. Doesn't he know what I've done? Doesn't he know how toxic I am, how volatile? Human beings aren't consistent, not even at being bad, yet he claims to love us.

But if God does see us, he sees us with greater clarity than we see. He can't be blind. His promises to us are given knowing all the risk. When he says "I love you" it must mean so much more than when I say it to someone. I'm saying it to someone who is just as polluted as me. There's some dark comfort in knowing that she's just as bad as me, just as unreliable and inconsistent. But God has no peers. He is perfect.

The very act of God promising me anything ennobles me and fills me with worth. I've always only ever been worthy of a human's love.

God's promises are different. He promises the son and the moon to us just like we promise to each other. The difference is, they're his to give.

twenty-four || meaning ii

Tell that to Jean-Paul Sartre, who said that "life has no meaning the moment you lose the illusion of being eternal." Maybe that's what this Christian thing is: an unwillingness to let go. Maybe I can't cope with the idea that there's nothing out there. I'm clinging to the edge of the branch, refusing to look down because I'm afraid of how high I've climbed up the tree. What if I fall?

What if there's nothing below? What if there's nothing *above*?

But how do you know for sure? Maybe life has meaning until you let go of the eternal. Maybe that's when it becomes meaningless. The idea that I'm wholly affected by my genes, that there's nothing I can do about who I am, is horrible. I don't want to be chained to the past. I want to be free. But to suggest that I can make my own way forward, regardless of the past, is hard to accept also. Maybe Sartre was scared to accept reality. Or maybe he was bold in declaring it. What I need is someone to judge between us. Somebody who's not affected by either genes or opinions to tell me what's going on. I want to know why I have questions.

twenty-five || when angels attack

God waited until he was alone before he attacked.

The anxiety encroached and grew bolder with each step Jacob took towards Edom. Four hundred armed men were on their way, and the best Jacob could do was divide up his family into two groups. That way, if the soldiers attacked one group at least part of Jacob's family would survive. A grizzly optimism at best.

Turn around. I'm sure that thought presented itself to Jacob over and over. *Why go towards Edom at all? It's not like Esau and his army were invading your lands, Jacob. You came to them, unarmed and with everything you owned.* But God had told Jacob to go back to Edom. For him, there was no going back.

Jacob was trapped between God and 400 armed men. Yet he pressed on with everything he owned and everyone he loved.

That's what it means to fear God more than men.

"So Jacob was left alone, and a man wrestled with him till daybreak."

Jacob had been praying to God, looking for some assurance that this would end well. He reminded God of the promises he made and even thanked God for everything he had done for him. But God didn't answer.

Still he prayed. Night swallowed up everything that was familiar and comforting to him on the other side of the river. He was totally alone.

But not quite alone. God appeared, disguised, and fought with Jacob. All night they pushed and punched and rolled around until the sun began to peek over the river bank. It was an even match, God and Jacob. But God fights dirty. "Let me go," God told him. But Jacob just held on all the harder. The tables were turned. God couldn't escape. So he touched Jacob's hip with a finger and bolts of pain shot through his body, but Jacob was a desperate man and still held on. That's when Jacob realized who he was fighting with.

"I'm not letting you go until you bless me," Jacob told God. Just a few hours earlier he had been thanking God for all the blessings he didn't deserve. Now he was fighting God for more.

You probably have a lot of time to think when you're wrestling with someone all night. Neither of them said anything to each other, and the frustrations of Jacob's life must have naturally bubbled to the surface. Twenty years ago, he had lied to his father, stolen from his brother, and schemed with his mother. He ran away from home a fugitive and was taken in—and taken advantage of—by the only family member around. But God was with him for some reason, and blessed him. It just wasn't enough. He was returning home now to the scene of the crime. He wasn't just facing his brother Esau again, he was facing his past. God can dole out sheep and servants all right, but Jacob had to know for sure that God had forgiven him. Maybe Jacob hadn't forgiven himself, either. But he needed some kind of assurance, and he was determined to get it. For only a man armed with guilty desperation can prevail against God.

Sometimes I wish God could come to wrestle with me too. Sometimes I wait for him by the river that flows through my back yard. Sometimes I want more than inaudible words. Sometimes I want to pin him to the ground and look in his eyes and see my desperation reflected there.

I deal with things too. I have doubts about my past. I would fight God for peace. To hold him down is just another way of holding on.

Sometimes it's hard to hold on to God.

Sometimes it just seems like he wants nothing more than to get away and escape back to where he came from.

Sometimes he makes holding on hurt.

Sometimes you have to hold on for a long time.

But daybreak comes.

twenty-six || woodstock

I feel like Joshua when he asked the Lord: "Are you on our side or their side?" and the Lord answered: "Neither." So often we ask the wrong questions.

I am inclined to agree with Paul Tillich that "theology formulates the questions implied in human existence." I studied theology and found that I was learning more about myself than about God.

I realized that I, too, was asking questions. Everybody is. The questions can be heard around us, though most don't realize it. Yet all of us eventually get around to asking the same question. And when you hear it you begin to realize that this is the task of all theology—to focus on the One Question.

It is everywhere. In the face of the smiling boy we hear, "Jesus, when can I play on your playground?" and in between sobs you can hear the woman asking God, "Why haven't you come yet?" and with each stroke the artist asks, "When will you show me *your* masterpiece, the art that doesn't just imitate life but gives it?" All this while (the other) Paul claims that every winter-weary maple leaf and orchid thirsts for the New Spring.

It is a concert of faith all around us.

To be so frail and temporary, so mortal, and yet consumed by an unnatural, immortal hunger leads me to doubt my doubts. *There has to be something more.* Everything in life points towards the conclusion. This hollowness was meant for holiness.

twenty-seven || expiration date

For some people it's too much. It's persistent agitation because they just have a heart to rebel against the order of things. They're like those who traveled with the children of Israel and whispered at every fork in the road: "Hey, why don't we go back to Egypt?" We'll always have people like this with us, people who only like the Promised Land of their dreams, people who wouldn't mind eternally traveling but never arriving. But we chase a real goal. We're going somewhere certain. If we waited for everyone to come to a consensus on every issue we'd never get anywhere. We travel by the Bible. We have a "thus says the Lord" to move us on. Stop fighting. Stop arguing. Stop wasting our time with this endless discussion.

To others it's not enough. It's a journey to understand, to make sure we get it right before we move on blindly, before we steamroll another crowd of would-be Christians with our that-settles-it-for-me (and for you) attitude. It's not about caution—about being unsure of ourselves—it's about compassion. Let's preach and teach the right things, but let's do it in the right way, too. When we are so eager to take things at face value and run ahead of God, are we really different from the history that we abhor? Are a thousand Christian Crusaders, so zealous to achieve the salvation they were promised at the expense of the "lost," really so different from a hundred church members being sent out to "work out their salvation" by informing people that "we're right and you're wrong"? Pointing swords or pointing fingers, blood is spilt either way. Stop fighting. Stop arguing. Stop wasting our time without discussion.

Sometimes I'm not sure who's right. Or, better yet, I know who I think is right, but I find it hard to say the other side is wrong. (Does that make any sense?) When truth is on both sides it can be dangerous not to sit on the fence. I don't harbor any illusions that one day we'll all agree on everything, but I think there is more still to be heard. Sure, we've all read the articles and heard the sermons. There are lots of them. Too many. At some point we have to stop and ask whether we're even talking to each other anymore, or only to our followers. It's like different halves of the family are discussing the same topic on opposite sides of the room. Stop fighting. Stop arguing. Stop wasting our time by pretending to discuss things.

Liberal. Conservative. Independent. Too bad the label also comes with a price sticker that tells others what you're worth. In the economy of ideas, your value depends on where you live and which other "products" you're next to. You get "scanned" every time you're asked a question about what you think about a hot issue. Then we know what aisle you've been stocked on.

Why does drawing a line make you draw a sword? It's essential to follow the Bible. But what does it mean when we can't follow the Bible…together?

twenty-eight || dreams

He dreamt of animals—four of them. One seemed to be something like a lion with the wings of an eagle. Another looked like a bear that drunkenly listed to port as it lumbered forward. By the time he saw the last beast, he couldn't compare it to anything. He simply said it was "terrifying and frightening and very powerful."

A little strange.

But he's not the only one, after all. I've dreamed I was at dinner with several ex-girlfriends at once. We all have nightmares.

This dream was different. Somehow, in this mister-potato-head vision of mixed-up animals, God encoded a detailed summary of the future.

It wasn't so romantic for Daniel. After the dream, Daniel admits that he felt "disturbed," "deeply troubled," and that his face turned "deathly pale." Later on, he confesses that he was "appalled by the vision" and felt sick for weeks. For five years, he wrestled with God to find out what all this meant. I'm sure he had lots of dreams in his life (they say the average person will have more than 200,000).But this one gripped him and wouldn't let go. He knew it was significant. He knew it meant something. He had to find out, and he

Daniel de Sevén || 59

gripped God with a desperate passion: "Lord, listen! Lord, forgive! Lord, hear and do something! For your sake, my God, do not delay."

All this for a dream?

All this for an encounter with God.

Daniel knew that when you find God—in those special moments where he really breaches our reality—you hold on to him, you fight for him as Jacob did. You seldom find him in the loud places of the world. You find him in dreams and in whispers and in the quiet places of life most of the time. You find him in the shadows. But once you find him, you can't let him go.

And holding on hurts. Daniel literally got sick. People thought he was going to die. It hurts to hold on to God. It was real. It wasn't just some spiritual exercise in the corner of a church. It took all of him to hold on as God kept telling him to wait a little longer. It's not easy. You can't decide to really follow God without committing yourself totally to it.

It defies reason. Put yourself in Daniel's shoes and try to explain any of this to someone. You're high up in the political architecture of a foreign, antagonistic power. Suddenly you grow ill and people start asking about you. What do you say? "Oh, well, God sent this dream which really bothers me and I've been praying really hard lately for him to explain it to me."

The reply is withering: "So you're sick because of a dream? And you think your god, whom we conquered when we carried you and your friends into captivity, sent you this dream? And he won't explain it to you? How many years have you been waiting again? Listen, man, it's time to move on." If someone came and told you this, would you believe them? Daniel had to seem totally out of his mind to everyone around him.

Or take Abraham. "God wanted you to secretly take your son out of his bed without telling anyone and travel three days so you could kill him for God on the top of some mountain?" Hello! What part of this plan sounds anything remotely like normal, rational behavior? Seriously, this is the type of stuff people often point to when they want to characterize religion as anti-reason or unhealthy.

You can go on and on, down the list: Noah, David, Ezekiel, Isaiah, Hosea, and others all did things that weren't just outside conventional wisdom, but outside of any sort of rational human behavior. We might be tempted to diagnose many of them with some mental or social disorder. Over and over God speaks to people in ways only they can understand. They can't prove it so that others will believe too. No one would understand. The person God speaks to is often very much alone. That's dangerous. But despite the insanity of it all, these are some of the most admired people in all of the Scriptures. And to them the crazy things that God asks make all the sense in the world. We all plead for God to speak to us in the cushioned comfort of our pews, and that's good. Most of the time he does and we walk away feeling "impressed" or "encouraged" or (more rarely) "convicted" about something or another. But how eager are we for God to really meet with us and let him tell us the something that is really on his heart? Can he really trust you?

God doesn't sit up there with everything figured out. His heart is gushing with things he wishes he could share with us! God, too, has needs and desires. The question is: are we willing to bear God's burdens? How many things God must want to tell us! Caution, though: it will weigh you down until your feet feel the flames of hell. But when the burden is lifted, you will breathe the sweet vapors of heaven itself.

You will have your moments sick in bed like Daniel. You will have your moments when the pain of holding on seems like it will kill you. You may be on your own, too. Those closest to you might think you're crazy. But then you will have your lion's dens too. You will have your moments when God shuts the mouths of lions for you just when you think it's all over. There will be times when he seems to tear down entire kingdoms for your sake. God fights ferociously for his closest friends.

All this in a dream?

All this in an encounter with God.

twenty-nine || ba'al

It seems that most of the people I know who have left Israel didn't do it because they thought Baal was better. They left because Yahweh—or one of his priests—has let them down. They left because they didn't find the Promised Land as it was promised.

Sometimes there are famines in Israel, and those who live on the border see first-hand how easy the life is of the people who don't have to carry sacrifices to the temple or pay a tenth of what they own. Their crops seem to grow just fine, despite the fact that they worship on the wrong day in the wrong way.

People look at the life and not the arguments. People want to see a life that is balanced, meaningful, and consistent. People will flock to the god who inspires that, regardless of its demands. As admirable as it is to see shepherds standing at the border crossings and trying to guarantee that people reason through their desire to immigrate (or emigrate), the decision to come or go is always made in the heart.

Christianity must have open borders.

thirty || wept

I didn't notice it before but maybe you have. Jesus lost one of his best friends. I guess it's comforting to know that even Jesus lost people close to him. It never baffled me that Jesus didn't run to Lazarus' bedside once he heard that he was sick. He waited a few days because he knew he could resurrect him from the dead. I think I would be the happiest person on earth if I had that kind of power. Why would people need to be sad? I'd heal everyone I could. There was no reason for anyone to cry. I'd walk cool and collected up to the casket and say, "Jeremy, get up!"

But it didn't happen that way with Jesus. Jesus walked up to the tomb all right, but then he stopped. What was he waiting for? I think he was praying. But if he was it didn't last long. Because then it says that Jesus wept. He cried. What did he have to cry about? He was about to raise his friend from the dead; why cry now? If anything, he should be comforting everyone with an arm around their shoulder, letting them know it's OK. But he cried.

It's confusing. My friend says she thinks he cried because of all the broken-hearted people around him. It just got to him. He was God and it got to him. That must mean something.

thirty-one || vivisection at the intersection

Belle and I stood at sixth and Michigan, when she drew my attention to a billboard of a model lying leisurely next to a bottle of wine.

"Do you think she personally likes that wine?" she asked. "I mean, I wonder if studies would demonstrate that models who personally approve of the product they are selling do a better job selling the product. You know, they express conviction or something."

"It may be," I replied. "But I don't see how conviction could be expressed in a still image."

"I think it could," she explained. "I think it manifests itself almost imperceptibly. You just see it or you don't, but you will never find a reason why you see it or why you can't."

"And a good thing, too! When marketers are able to choreograph conviction I'd say we have lost something very human."

"What do you mean?" she asked. It was her turn to need explanation.

"Doesn't it occur to you that these billboards are themselves a very inhuman thing? What you see is not a woman, but an image designed to look like a woman. In fact, with the way camera technology is, she may look quite similar to the real thing. Yet we always refer to these images as "she" and "he" rather than "it." We treat them as if they are real people. In reality, they are objectifications."

"Objectifications?" Belle looked at me curiously.

"Yes, that image is meant to convey luxury, accessibility, affluence, beauty, sexual attractiveness, etc. This is what they determined will help them sell a bottle of wine. So they tell this woman to dress this way and act according to these 'ideals' so that they can sell this bottle. They don't want the woman, they want the ideals. It's objectification of a person. That's why they have her sign all these papers giving them the 'rights' to her 'image' and so forth."

"So," Belle said, "people will go out and buy this product because they want what this represents, what it values? Yet they can't pick any person. They have to choose a person who best represents these values. So in a sense—though not in a physical sense perhaps—it is an accurate description of her—a person."

"Are you sure?" I said. "Today there is a certain standard of luxury and attractiveness, but it may change tomorrow. Tomorrow she could find her career over because she no longer exudes the ideal. She can't sell the kind of things people want to sell. This is the real tragedy of the whole affair. They call her a model. Why not call her a mannequin? 'Your job,' they might tell them, 'is to stand here and behave like this inanimate object.' Except this model is meant to demonstrate a certain definition which may change at any time. Her usefulness is wrapped up in the capitalistic winds or constrained by age. Except she cannot change the way she looks (though many try), so it is unfortunate when things do change. What was her legacy? What impact did she have on society?"

"I see," she said. "It is rather like taxidermy. She used to be living but they killed her and displayed her on this board because they think she makes a pretty rug by the fire. What an undignified thing to do to someone. It is sick."

"Yes," I agreed, glancing one last time at the board before crossing the street. "It is rather like a tombstone, except she has no beautiful lines to commemorate her. She only has a bottle of wine."

"And we don't even know if she liked it," Belle added.

thirty-two || existence precedes essence

"We are part and parcel of the whole," Rabbit explained. "And that's why freedom is such a childish notion."

Grasshopper thought for a very long time, and then replied: "But I want to be free."

Rabbit laughed. "You are never free. You are tied to the thoughts of your parents, the culture of your family, and the socio-economic conditions of your neighborhood. You can do nothing wholly original, nothing authentically creative. You are a product of everything, a child of the world. We all had a hand in who you turned out to be."

Grasshopper looked sullen, and Rabbit rejoiced. His pupil was finally understanding.

"But I want to be free. Surely that counts for something?"

thirty-three || nietzsche judged

"What will they say about me, when my age has passed? How will I be received?"

"You will be judged."

"Really? By whom?"

"By your children."

"Yet I am the judge, the judge who proved that no one is even-handed enough to deserve to be judge. I thought I handed this virtue down to my children."

"You did, and it was precisely because there was no judge that they were incarcerated anyway."

"They judge me then because I took away their judges, those men in pompous wigs prattling on about duty trying to organize the world into neat columns?"

"You will be judged because you smiled at their deceit, finding no small amusements in their subtle tricks. You are judged because you had the truth and called it a lie; you had the truth and you were not gentle in applying it. In the end, you were not true at all."

thirty-four || two worlds

We raise our cubicle walls high against the Montana sky. These emaciated boundaries form the confines of our world. We can touch it, feel it, experience it—it protects us from the vast, untamed expanse around us. It protects us from what we don't know and fear to guess.

But how absurd we look in this modern Babel, with these manufactured walls (which are so natural to us) saving us from these wise rocks, peaceful fields, and laughing sky. We've left the garden and never looked back. Here we are, claiming to master this borrowed space. But we never look at it from the outside.

thirty-five || thief

Jesus is a thief.

Sure he is Lord, King, Savior, Father, and Priest as well. But he is also a thief.

"I will come like a thief," he tells us in Revelation, "and you will not know at what time I will come to you."

Question: What kind of thief warns his victims that he is coming?

Apparently, Jesus isn't a very good thief.

Maybe that's the point.

He's coming back, and he knows that most people aren't looking for him. So he tells us that he wants us to be watching. Fair enough, but why compare yourself to a thief? Why not just say, "I'm going to drop by at any time, so keep the house clean"?

Maybe it's because we have such strong emotional reactions towards thieves. We're protective of our things and our family, and thieves violate and threaten us. They undermine our sense of confidence and security. Like it or not, that's kind of how the Second Coming will be. It's not a friendly visit. It invades your space. All of us, even the ones who want Jesus to come, have put down roots here. We've got a routine going. The Second Coming is change; needed change, but radical change.

Nothing will be safe. Every eye will see Jesus, the Scriptures tell us, and, conversely, Jesus will see every eye. We can't hide anything from him. We can't protect anything from him. "I am coming," he says, "and my reward is with me." It's time to settle accounts. God can't be resisted any longer. No more idle philosophizing. No more fence-sitting. He is coming.

Jesus isn't describing his actions or motives when he calls himself a thief, he is describing the reality of his coming to people who think their lives are locked up and secure. Whatever gives us a feeling of safety will be torn open and exposed. We can't possibly imagine what it will be like for our whole flow of time to be so suddenly cut off at his arrival. And it's clear that he doesn't want people to be surprised because he warns us—all of us. We ought to be apprehensive of it. There are so many things that are unknown. No one, not even believers, will really be able to say they are prepared for his coming, like a soldier in boot camp cannot really say he is prepared for war. But it's not a bad thing. It's the best thing. After all, what kind of thief warns us he is coming?

One who wants to be caught by you.

thirty-six || ready (or not)

Our little kingdoms fall. We wonder: why did we think these walls were so tall? Why were we so intimidated by stone and steel? There were giants all around us the whole time and we never realized it. We feel naked and exposed, shamed at having made so much of ourselves when we are now seen as so much less.

People are running everywhere. Some are running from him; some are running to him.

Him...

Jesus.

Tell me how you can be ready for that. You can read your Bible every day and pray and all that, but something tells me this is one thing you can't really prepare yourself for. It's lodged in my mind—Jesus is coming soon. I got it. I can show it to someone in the Bible. I can preach with passion about it. But on some level, I know I can never really be ready for it.

But Jesus told us to be ready. Over and over again. He said things like, "watch and pray" and to "be vigilant." He expects us to be ready. But how can we be ready?

I remember one of the numerous Nerf wars I had in the basement of my house growing up. My friends and I would turn off all of the lights and set up barricades of clothes baskets, boxes of Christmas stuff, and who knows what else in order to shield ourselves from the impending onslaught of darts and arrows from the other team. Did I mention it was dark? We really couldn't see three feet in front of us. It was awesome.

But then we had to wait. We held perfectly still, afraid to breathe, listening to every little sound that might give us a clue as to where our enemy was, because we had no idea when the darts would start flying and we didn't want to get caught unprepared.

Is that how Jesus expects us to wait, frozen in fear and perpetually peering over the parapets we hide behind? That may be necessary in times of extreme crisis, but no one can keep up that kind of adrenaline-inspired vigilance for very long. It's exhausting. You can't live that way.

So what are we supposed to do? How do you prepare for such a thing as the return of Jesus? Aren't we already prepared by virtue of being a Christian and being saved?

It may be an obvious point to make, but Jesus tells us to be ready because he knows there's a chance we won't be ready. It's not alarmism; it's reality. And yet I doubt it for some reason. Something in me whispers, "Look, life is going great. I feel like a conspiracy theorist preparing for persecution in an age of peace and tolerance." It doesn't seem like it could happen.

But Jesus knows it will, and so he wants us to be prepared. It doesn't mean we have to wear sandwich board signs declaring that the end is near. We don't have to cut out newspaper headlines or—horror—watch C-SPAN 24/7 to make sure Congress isn't trying to slip something by us. That's not what being prepared means.

We must realize that Jesus is warning us for a reason, and a quick trip through Matthew 24 gives us an idea of what will be going on just before he comes: there will be a lot of fighting in the world, a decline in morality, persecution of people who claim to be Christians, and natural disasters on an unprecedented scale.

Some of these things aren't that exciting to us. There have always been wars and disease, so we don't know exactly what makes this occasion so unique, except that they might be worse. But the big picture is that our world will be turned upside down. Jesus drives the point home when he says, "If those days had not been cut short, no one would survive."

And the thing that Jesus seems most concerned about is the fact that people will come claiming to be on his side who aren't. "Many false prophets will appear and deceive many people," he says. Between persecution of Christians and those falsely claiming to be Christians, God's people will be caught in the crossfire. And Jesus wants us to know what's going on so that we can brace ourselves for it. I think most Christians expect Jesus to just show up one day and it'll all be over. But he doesn't tell us that. He says it's going to get bad before it gets worse, and he wants us to know so that we can have confidence in him.

Think about it. How many people become disillusioned and want to give up on marriage because it wasn't what they expected? Maybe they thought it'd be easy, and when it turns out that they are incessantly fighting with their newly-minted spouse for the first three months they want out, or at least think about it. On the other hand, if you expect marriage to have challenges, then when they come you're not caught off-guard. They may not be fun, but they're part of the process, and that's okay. Likewise, Jesus warns us ahead of time so we know that he is still in control. All of it isn't going to take God by surprise, so it shouldn't be a surprise to us either. On the contrary, when it happens we should have even greater confidence in God, as bad as it may be. The prophecies are less about providing us with markers so we can figure out when it will happen than a confidence-boost when we realize these things are coming true.

It's kind of like getting directions from a friend where he tells you to turn right at the giant ceramic pig and then go until you see a gas station and take a left. You may see all sorts of things and wonder where on earth your friend is telling you to go, but when you see the giant pig you'll feel good because you're on the right course.

So Jesus' warnings give us confidence that when the world turns upside down we should believe that things are finally going right side up. But there is also a real danger. He says that false prophets are going to come. Now prophets aren't just people in robes who predict the future. Prophets are people who have a deep relationship with God and tell people what God wants to say. Some predict the future, but very few; most are concerned with the present. What Jesus fears is that Christians will turn to listen to these people who claim to speak for God. But Jesus didn't tell us to ignore all prophets. He only told us to be on guard against the false ones. That implies that there will be real people who speak for God. That makes it vital that we learn to discern between the two.

And that is something we can be ready for. We can be ready by immersing ourselves in the Scriptures and seeking God frequently in our daily lives. As we interact with him each day and learn to hear his voice, then we will know when a person speaks for God and when he doesn't. Then we won't be deceived. We will remain on the right side.

We can be ready by listening to Jesus in the daily things while remembering what this is all about. What's the point of being ready if we forget what we're getting ready for? So we have to stay in the Scriptures and remind ourselves not just what is going to happen but what has happened in the past. All the while we have to keep in mind that the real focus isn't on deception, persecution, or turmoil, but on the hope of the Second Coming. Being ready is about looking for a future renewal, and inviting it to start now. In faith we look forward to a new life and prepare by beginning to live it today.

Section III
Therefore I AM

thirty-seven || disguised

The Israelites who left Egypt were stoked. I mean, they had seen their god return after 400 years of being silent. 400 years. That would be like not hearing from God since the 1600s. And just like that, he worked miracle after miracle in plain sight of the entire nation as he delivered his people from captivity. Then they were at the base of this mountain and everything was going great. They agreed to enter into a "marriage" with this god who saves people. And why not tie your future to a god like that?

But on the third day their optimism melted as this god touched the mountain. Suddenly there was thunder and lightning and earthquakes and fire all around. Suddenly this god was too close. Suddenly he was too real to them. He was much safer up in heaven (wherever that was) where he could just send a cloud ahead of them to show the way. The god of the mountain was terrifying.

Sometimes it's just safer to keep God in heaven. As long as he points the way and delivers us from our own Egypts we're happy. But when he wants to come close it's a different matter. We have a god who is a little scary up close. He's the god who causes storms and also sleeps through them. He's the god who throws over the very tables he carved. He's the god who disappears when people are looking for him and claims he wants to be found by those who aren't. He's not one of us.

We prefer him in a disguise. Oh sure we want him to come and rescue us, but as a carpenter from Nazareth and not as the god from heaven. We plead with him to save us, but as a calmer of the seas and not as an angel with a flaming sword. Sacrificial lambs are much safer than untamed lions. Who wouldn't rather hang the cross on the wall than be the one hanging on the cross?

Maybe that's why I have such a hard time picturing Jesus walking my streets. I just can't see him in cargo shorts and a t-shirt talking about cars with my friends. I really can't imagine a parable about a squirrel or Jesus escaping to the Rocky Mountains to pray. My Jesus doesn't know what a movie theater is (and doesn't know when I go).

No, my imagination won't let him get that close to me. It's safer this way. All the while he wears that familiar robe he's somewhere else, locked in another century that we only visit on weekends.

But I know I need to change. I know God, but only the part of him that's safe. He wants me to know him more completely—yes, even the part of him that terrifies me. Otherwise, do I really know him? Or do I only know the god I made out of my own imagination?

Sometimes graven images are made without hands.

thirty-eight || therefore I AM

"My God," he cried. "Why have you abandoned me?"

This is Jesus, whom we cling to in all our insecurities as the example, the standard. I was the one bailing water out of the boat while he slept safely astern. I was panicked, and yet comforted that my deepest fears didn't so much as rouse him. He was unflappable, courageous, always pressing forward so I could follow.

But now, doubt?

If anyone in history was ever confident that God was with them it was Jesus. If anyone had more evidence or greater faith it was him. And yet at the end of all things he dared to confess his doubt.

And everyone heard.

It wasn't just that he thought it. He said it. He called out to God through all the jeering and weeping. "Why have *you* abandoned me? God, I am still here. Where have *you* gone to hide from me?"

His Father wasn't gone, of course. Jesus just

couldn't feel that connection with him anymore. Jesus became blind.

His broken heart broke the earth beneath him. The sky grew dark even as Jesus confessed that he could not see. But next to him came the Father's voice from an unexpected prophet:

"Surely this man was the Father's Son!"

A Roman centurion, callous and calculating, together with a thief, were the only ones to offer any affirmation. They alone saw that the Father hadn't abandoned the Son after all.

But Jesus was already dead. It was finished.

And a pierced side showed the world He was just like one of us after all. His heart harbored the same faith and the same doubts, which poured out together in the blood and the water.

It was the price for blasphemy. He had said to the world, "Before Abraham, before the law, before Adam himself, I AM! Before your traditions and your heroes, I was there. I was the one who first brought death into the world when I killed a lamb for your first parents. I was the angel with the sword of flame, hoping that through its terror and brightness you wouldn't see the tears I cried as I took the tree of life from you. I was the one who pardoned the first murderer, and murdered an entire world for the sake of eight. I AM the one who spoke on Sinai, at whose voice Moses drew closer while the nation trembled. I brought manna down from heaven each morning to feed you in the desert, and I am that bread even today. I have come out to you upon the dew to feed those who are hungry. But I was only greeted by the fawn and the dove. My son, why have you forsaken me?"

But he returned. Somehow—who can say for sure—he walked away from death into a brighter day. It was as if to say: "if God can resolve the problem of death, can't he deal with my problems, too?"

"My Lord and my God!" Thomas exclaimed to the resurrected Savior. "I believe you now. I have no more doubts that you are who you say you are!"

Jesus smiled. "Blessings upon those who weren't here to see me and still believe."

"Because even after all your doubts, I AM."

thirty-nine || ravine

The man said to Jesus: "Lord, I believe! Help me with my doubts! I so desperately want to believe!"

And Jesus wept at his honesty.

"Truly," said He, "man stands on a pillar in the midst of a great ravine. Whichever direction he wishes to go he must leap to get there. Leap to me, my son, and we will walk together. Only then will you be satisfied."

The man looked at his feet and, seeing solid ground in the few feet between him and Jesus, leaped anyway.

forty || jealousy

Our God is a jealous god. He is possessive—a green-eyed monster.

Jealousy, some say, is so unbecoming.

But the battered, the wounded, and broken-hearted are running *towards* him. All around me. They say his eyes drew them in. They say jealousy is a good thing.

How can jealousy be a good thing?

Solomon saw jealousy as part of who God is: "For [His] love is as strong as death; [His] jealousy as unyielding as the grave."

Some of the gods people have believed in are jealous, too. The Greek goddess Hera, was jealous of the women her husband, Zeus, seemed to prefer over her. She turned one into a bear, and another into a monster after murdering her children. In another case she sent her henchmen to eat one of Zeus' children. Yeah, "hell hath no fury…" and all of that.

The message was clear to every believer: you don't make the gods jealous.

Yet the God of the Israel is proud of being jealous. Solomon saw God's love and his jealousy as the same. There was no difference. He was proud of being jealous. And yet he didn't act like those other gods. When he accused his people of cheating on him—like Hera accused to Zeus of doing—he didn't tear them limb for limb. He was angry like any of us would be, but his love always smothered his anger.

When we say that we're jealous, we usually mean that we're envious or bitter about something. But God has nothing to envy us about. He is jealous for us, not of us. It's a subtle difference. Being jealous for us means that he fights on our behalf, even when we don't realize it or appreciate it.

Imagine your daughter walking into work at the office. Assuming that this is not strange at all, you down an invisibility potion and follow her in. Then you notice what some of the people are thinking: (uh…you apparently also drank a mind-reading potion. Where do you get these things?) one guy wonders what she'd look like without that blouse. Another girl rolls her eyes and thinks that she looks like a prostitute. Not everyone thinks bad things, of course, but its enough to make you want to throw off the gloves and intervene.

God wants our good for us. It seems strange, I know. But that's how it is. Even when we don't want the good, he does.

Jealous.

forty-one || dirge

"We played the pipe for you and you did not dance; We sang a dirge and you did not mourn."
                             - Matthew 11:17

This Jesus said because he knew their hearts. "When the Son of Man is laid lifeless, the heavens will break with grief while you rejoice in mirth. But when the Son of Man returns to his Father in triumph you will weep while the angels laugh. I tell you the truth, for despite all your complexity a man's heart is clearly discerned by what he chooses to laugh at and what he chooses to cry over. But follow me; stay awake and weep with me while I weep and I promise you will smile with me while I smile. Then I will know that you are my disciples indeed."

forty-two || snakes

I don't know about you, but snakes wouldn't have been my first sign. With all the power of the cosmos in my hands and the desire to set my people free, I would have chosen something…grander.

Don't get me wrong, it's a wonderful story: Moses and Aaron standing before Pharaoh, demanding that he let a couple of million slaves simply walk out of the country just because they said "please." Then Pharaoh laughs in their faces, and it evolves into a battle between two persistent men and their gods.

And what does the Hebrew God do for his opening salvo? Snakes. Aaron throws his staff to the ground and it transforms into a snake. It's a scary thing to think I can do something better than God, but had he asked me to brainstorm with him I might have suggested writing his name in fire high in the sky or giving all the Egyptians a tattoo that says, "I AM God, you are wrong." But, snakes?

Even more bizarre is the fact that the Egyptian religious leaders could do the same thing. Is this a common thing to do? Did I somehow miss this class in school? It seems rather strange that people knew how to do this. But it wasn't just snakes, however. These Egyptians were able to replicate the first *three* miracles that God worked.

It's easy to get all preachy here. It's easy to look at this as that great battle of good and evil, between the ones who work miracles on behalf of God and the ones who work miracles on the side of Satan. Each time they were able to counterfeit God's miracles, Pharaoh was confirmed in his decision.

But something interesting happens when we encounter the fourth miracle. This time God sends gnats to annoy all of Egypt and the magicians have to admit to Pharaoh that "this is the finger of God." Strangely enough, Pharaoh's magicians were honest. They recognized the limits of their power and faithfully told their boss that they couldn't do it. After that, they're out of the story.

It's a curious thing that often those people who are working directly to discredit us aren't really our enemies. We don't need to be so naïve as to think that Pharoah's magicians then converted and served the Jewish God, but we can say that, steeped in the religion and rites of Egypt, they were open enough to admit that the other team was better. It tells me that I need to be careful about who I consider my enemy. Maybe they're just as sincere as I am. Sometimes the people we consider to be "snakes" are just waiting to be used by God.

forty-three || DH905569

"Your name shall no longer be called Jacob, but Israel; for you have struggled with God and with men, and have prevailed."
- Gen. 32:28.

A name, not a number. That's what we all prefer. But sooner or later, we find that we're just one of the crowd. Part of a statistic where we make up a percentage used to describe a whole that never existed. People cannot become numbers without ceasing to be human.

And so there exists among us many inhuman humans. They are like a scientist and we are their mice. They are people who have betrayed people by viewing them as numbers. We have one thought, one opinion, and all policy is bent to cater to "what the people want." The people want more than one thing. I am more than my political views, more than my beliefs. I'm more than what you made me out to be.

But I am here to declare the emancipation of humanity. I am here to give names back to the numbered.

forty-four || she is

We are nothing. But you and I seem to think that we matter. There are endless ways in which we build ourselves up, attributing great meaning to each milestone on our slow march into nonexistence. We build towering memorials to each other in an attempt to grant ourselves the immortality that we've already forfeited. While eternity, an ethereal stream, flows overhead, just out of reach but not out of sight. It is the curse of our bent race.

But it is our blessing also. With lustful curiosity we tore open Pandora's jar, and somehow through the flood of evils we unleashed, Hope remained. But Hope, if it was to remain hope at all, could not stay at the bottom. So Hope was born like one of us, and drew all our despair to Herself. Hope perished beneath the blackness of our sky and, rumored reborn, rose to become the Sun that forever chases the shadow away.

We used to have to try so hard. We enshrined the bravest warriors, the richest men, the wisest philosophers. We deified those who created conveniences for the problems invented by yesterday's gods. To live forever in the collective consciousness you had to stand out of the crowd. You had to be somebody unique among a race of unique people. You had to be more than human or else you were forgotten (and that truly is the second death).

But no longer. Our great biographies are eulogies of a dream we now dread. Now Hope lives among us as daylight grows bolder with each passing day. Still, many reach deep into the old jar for a new hope. They think the story can be unwoven and retold until it gives them a better role to play. But they grasp in vain. Only shadows remain at the bottom of the jar, the last place where despair is permitted to remain.

The truth is more beautiful. The light pierces our predilection of self-perfection. It humbles us. It fills us with pride.

Suddenly I am worth something.

I am worth more than I ever pretended.

forty-five || empty

The cross and the coming were never too far apart. Jesus taught us to pray, "Thy kingdom come." We're supposed to want it, to expect it, to pray for him to come even while we ask for forgiveness and help through the day. We are to look for Christ to come as the first followers were told to look for an empty tomb.

The power of the cross was not simply in Jesus dying under a brooding sky, but in the vacant grave as well. For the resurrection was power. It showed us that nothing could hold God back from us. Death, our strongest foe, has broken our human ties and reversed God's creation. It has never let us go or shown us mercy. Rather, death stalks us, hunting us down in so many clever, creative ways. But the life and love of Jesus Christ prevailed. It was easy for the man Jesus to die—everybody dies—but for him to return from the grave gives us hope that we can return from our fallen places. Jesus proved that he is strong enough to overcome whatever prevents us from returning home with him. And not only is he strong enough, but he showed us that he's willing as well.

The resurrection was a promise too. It showed us our future and what God planned to do for us. It was a foretaste of the Second Coming, a trailer to the main event. So why do we pretend the resurrection is in the past? Isn't it in our future as well? Doesn't it have as much to do with the Second Coming as with the cross?

We often treat salvation as if it's something that's behind us now. You and I, we are not saved. Look at where we are. Did not the apostle say, "Do not grieve the Holy Spirit of God, with whom you were sealed for the day of redemption"? In one sense we are saved, in that we are "sealed" or marked by God to be saved. In that way we have our ticket, but we are not riding yet. It would be pointless if salvation only meant going to church and trying to be a better person. There's more to it than that. That's just the beginning. We are not yet home, and it would be a grave mistake to settle down here as if this is the life you were saved for. This isn't what you were meant for. The empty tomb teaches you that. It happened to remind you that just because Jesus is gone it doesn't mean it's over now.

While sin is a tragic detour from God's original plan, it has enabled us to experience him in a way we never would have been able to otherwise. At Easter many Christians sing the words: "*O felix culpa quae talem et tantum meruit habere redemptorem*" or "O happy fault that merited such and so great a Redeemer." It seems wrong on some level to be thankful for this situation. But it's okay. It's one of those cases where we realize that it's something we'd never do again, but we're thankful for what we saw and learned in the process. It's God's way to bring good things out of the bad. That doesn't change the fact that it's still bad, but unexpected blessings often bloom in these situations. That's what God does.

The cross. The tomb. The coming. It's all one smooth brush stroke. It's all part of the process of redeeming people. It's been in God's mind the whole time. The last feast that the Hebrew people were called to celebrate was the Festival of Tabernacles. On that day the people were asked to live in tents or some kind of temporary structure to remind them of how they were wanderers in a barren place before God had led them to a new home in the Promised Land. They were also told to cut palm branches and wave them in the air and rejoice in God that they were in a new land. Can you imagine what that must have looked like? Can you imagine what it must have sounded like? An entire nation gathered together celebrating the fact that God had led them home!

An entire nation…

An entire church…

forty-six || home

Where did you think this was going?

To so many it's just the hobbyhorse of those Christians who lack deep roots in history. The younger faith communities seem more easily excitable, jumping up and down and waving signs that say the end is near. They say things like, "Jesus is coming soon" and preach with great fire. But inevitably their passion dies down, tempered by time.

The early church thought Jesus was coming soon. It was a huge part of their conversation. The disciples wrote as if Jesus would come in their lifetime. But eventually that faded away as other problems arose. Reformers like Martin Luther thought it would take place in their lifetime. But eventually the idea subsided as the Reformation went on. Even in our time there are many groups who have tried to set dates for Jesus to return or have simply tried to keep the advent hope alive in their congregations.

Christian communities that have been around for a while know it's not so easy to maintain this hope. Jesus doesn't come because we want him to. He has defied all of our expectations. At first, it seems like the easy way out to embrace this advent hope. I can avoid wrestling with the questions posed by modern science, taking a stand on hot ethical topics, and worrying about the consequences of quitting my job because Jesus is coming soon. No need to pay back that loan, fix up the house, or save for college, it'll all be over soon. But it's hard to hold on. It's hard to maintain momentum in the reality that generations pass away without Jesus showing up.

Some people ignore the fact that he is coming. Or they take it to the other extreme and pretend he has already come. Many of us fall under the first group. It's not that we don't believe Jesus is coming, it's just a little awkward trying to live like he's coming. It's a piece of our faith we're afraid to share with others. We ask: "What can we do about it now, anyway? Just try to live your life as best you can, according to God's will, and whenever Jesus does come you'll be fine."

On the other side, some Christians see Jesus' return as a reason to distance themselves from the rest of the world. It's a time to focus on getting ready to meet him, cutting away the unnecessary entertainment and the compromises of comfort that we are all prone to make. It's a time to take faith more seriously and look for ways to alert people to our perilous time in earth's history. It's totally opposite from the first approach in that it asks: "What more can I do to get myself ready?"

Truthfully, with each approach comes some good

and some bad. It's impossible to be confronted with the reality of the second coming and insist that it has nothing to do with life today. Likewise, it's rather contradictory to use it as an excuse to separate ourselves from the world. It's just there, and we must wrestle with it.

If anything, the reality that Jesus is coming should make Christians *more* responsible and *more* willing to engage the people around them. We are inspired to right wrongs we have committed, to tell others that the final act of redemption is near, and to develop our gifts so that we can bless others. Those believers who constantly affirm the hereafter should be the most effective at making a difference in the here and now. The Second Coming is the physical realization of the Gospel call: the kingdom of God is here!

Belief in what Paul calls "the blessed hope" shouldn't be lost with time or tradition. This hope is part of the redemption story; it didn't end with the cross. Revelation shows us a picture of an angel flying in the sky "having the everlasting gospel" and declaring that Jesus is near. John saw an intimate connection between the coming of Jesus and spreading the good news of salvation. To subdue this hope or to take it as an excuse to avoid sharing the Gospel is to miss the purpose of our Christianity—to go home and invite as many people as we can along the way. After all, we haven't been working these 2,000 years just so we can build more churches and hospitals. Where are you going in your Christianity, if not home? So let the Advent Hope radiate in your life.

"In that day they will say: This is truly our God, we trusted him and he saved us. This is the Lord, we trusted him, so we rejoice in his salvation!

He will swallow up death forever. The Sovereign Lord will wipe away every tear from our faces and remove his children's sadness from all the earth."

forty-seven || romance of the divine

X

Lust burns, smolders, and mugs passion for her dream. It is to steal what can only be given.

So why are you—you who would never dare to lust in this sphere—so consumed by this god-lust? Why do you crave his blessing to get you out of this fix? After you've had your fill, will you stick around? After you get that job, that wife—that life—will you wake up with the same prayer on your lips?

Or are you only in it for a moment? (For in a moment we are all changed!) Love, not lust, is the keeper of sacred trust. Maybe your profession of undying love speaks more to a need behind your lie. You may rob God of the moment's pleasure, but you will be unfulfilled if you walk away. It's never as easy as it looks. You won't be able to get him out of your head.

He'll call you, you know. Just when you thought you got a clean get-a-way he'll find you in the yellow pages or stop by your favorite restaurant when you're at lunch. He'll expect more. He'll want what you promised him. And just when you thought your one-Sunday stand was safely hid behind that snickering smile, he'll disappear…and you'll feel the loss.

X

You chanced his love and found it stronger than you could bear. It suffocated you and you feared death in his arms. You got more than you bargained for because you don't bargain with God. He has only one price.

Why does the liar distrust everyone? Why does he see the world as dishonest? Because he has made the world what he wants it to be. He has fashioned it out of his imagination, and placed his heart in the Soul of the World.

Yet God imagines us differently.

God said of you: "I have loved you with an everlasting love. I have called you, and you are mine." What is his he keeps and cherishes. He takes nothing for granted.

But you are he who said: "For, though I knew His love who followed, yet I was sore adread, lest, having Him, I must have naught beside." God said it would cost you far more to maintain your shackles than to embrace your freedom. You rankled your chains in defiance.

And God smiled at your anguish, knowing that "fear wist not to evade as love wist to pursue."

forty-eight || fifteen years

Another one of those deathbed prayers: just a little more time; one more day without pain. After all, he reasoned, didn't he deserve it?

The Assyrians were wicked. Notoriously wicked. In the whole of the ancient world, there was no one like them. But Hezekiah had stood up to them and God was with him. The Assyrians were destroyed. It was the only battle the Assyrian king Sennacherib ever lost.

But Hezekiah grew terminally ill. It was a cruel twist of fate—surviving a siege but dying from disease. The heroic Hezekiah would die in agony, alone.

"Remember, Lord," he prayed, "how I have walked before you faithfully and with wholehearted devotion have done what is good in your eyes." Clearly he didn't think this was fair, either. The same verse tells us that he wept in bitterness.

For whatever reason, Hezekiah's attempt to remind God of how great a friend he was worked, and God granted him fifteen more years of life.

Did he really deserve it?

When he was all better and loving his new lease on life, the crown prince of Babylon—Hezekiah's former allies against Assyria—decided to make a visit and congratulate him on his miraculous recovery. Hezekiah decided to give him the grand tour, showing him all the gold and weapons and nice things he had laying around. Maybe Hezekiah had forgotten that Sennacherib had rampaged through Mesopotamia, looting every city he touched—cities like Babylon.

So maybe it wasn't the shrewdest move, showing a starving lion all the food you have. A hundred years later, it was Babylon's turn to knock on Jerusalem's door. *Say, remember all that stuff you showed us...*

But back to Hezekiah. The prophet Isaiah popped in after the prince of Babylon left and let into him. "How can you be so dumb?" was the gist of what he said. "Some day they're going to come back and attack you and nothing will be left. Everything will be wiped out."

"Oh well," Hezekiah replied. "At least there will be peace and security in my lifetime." *Not my problem.*

How could a person who went through so much with God—who was miraculously saved and then healed—turn out to be so ungrateful?

When Sennacherib was in the neighborhood Hezekiah ran to the Temple: "Lord, I need your help here!" After all, his life was at stake. When he found out he was going to die, he turned to the Lord and said, "Lord, I need your help here!" After all, his life was at stake. But when he was told that his moment of pride would mean the destruction of the same city he had fought so valiantly to save, he shrugged. *Not my problem.*

Why aren't you running into the Temple this time, Hezekiah? Why not turn your face to God and ask him for help again?

Can't you even try? How hard is it to pray?

I guess it's different when your life isn't on the line anymore.

God gifted Hezekiah fifteen years—to the eternal envy of anyone who has ever uttered one of those deathbed prayers.

But Hezekiah used those fifteen years to ensure that not only would Jerusalem inevitably be destroyed, but that the Jewish nation would never again be free for over 2,500 years.

But it wasn't his problem…

forty-nine ‖ three movements

I saw her, standing, smiling…but not at me. No, not yet.

Something about her changed the atmosphere of the room. I had a good job, close friends… but for some reason I felt incomplete. It wasn't enough. She stole my happiness and, yet, seemed to promise it in return.

In return for what?

An encounter…
    Just a glance. Maybe a smile. No words.

But it couldn't end there. It wasn't enough. There could be no limits. It was insane, but how could I ever forgive myself if I didn't investigate? Her very presence robbed me of all my accomplishments. I was starting over again.

I felt her eyes on me. I looked down, hoping she wouldn't see that the family room was a mess.

I knew she was smiling, I could feel it like the sun bursting through the clouds.

    Then words, silence, dinner, smiles…

    "Let's give it a shot…"

Slowly my confidence returned, but it was different now.

   I wasn't the same. I was changing.

She wasn't trying to change me; it just happened.

   Or maybe she was?

I learned so much about her, and yet she never ceased to surprise and delight me. I dove head-first, knowing that the waves were only on the surface.

She was so disarming and I didn't know how to act without the security of my sarcasm, my criticism, my stereotypes, or my disdain for the truly "other."

How does one live life without weapons?

It was love.
   And she said "yes."

"Yes" was a new summit to climb and yet it carried with it the perils of the descent.

I had a new paradigm for happiness; a new source.

She made me want to be more like myself than I had ever been. I was home. I was "me" at last.

fifty || vicar

We are his representatives. We are his people. We are his children.

Joseph's brothers got tired of his dreams and threw him in a well. Have you ever been held accountable for your dreams? It's like people expect us to be able control what we dream about. The other night I dreamt I was flying in a plane, then suddenly I was having a huge dinner with hundreds of other people (they served Little Debbie snacks for dessert), and finally I was walking down this staircase when a woman I know did something to irritate me. I woke up really mad at her; it seemed so real. Even though I knew it was a dream, I was angry when I saw her later in the day. Was it her fault I dreamt that she did what she did? Was it mine?

I'm sure Joseph's brothers assumed what so many do: "For Joe to dream that we all bow down to him means he's been thinking about it a lot. How arrogant can he be?"

Yeah, I don't think about Little Debbie's. I mean, seriously.

So the story worked out and Joseph, as you know, became a ruler in Egypt and everybody made up. But after Joseph's father, Jacob, died his brothers were concerned again, wondering if Joseph will use this opportunity to get revenge. So they sent messengers to Joseph and said, "Uh, yeah, please don't hurt us."

Joseph wept. "Am I God?" he asked incredulously. It's like Joseph read *The Lord of the Rings* (or at least J.R.R. Tolkien read Joseph): "Many that live deserve death. And some that die deserve life. Can you give it to them? Then be not too eager to deal out death in the name of justice." So elegant.

But, man, how many times do I play God? Joseph had every right to fix his brothers good for what they did to him. They left him to die—*their own flesh and blood!* In the ancient near east, family was everything. You didn't hurt your family, no matter how annoying they were. Furthermore, Joseph had become second-in-command of Egypt. He had the power, and no one would have blamed him.

But we kind of know what Joseph will do because, earlier in his life when he was a slave, his master's wife put on that seductive mango scent and tried to lure him into bed. He had the power, and no one would have blamed him. After all, that's what any "healthy" male would have done, right? Not Joseph. "How can I do this wickedness against God?" he asked of her. (I presume he actually wasn't interested in a reply.)

That's Joseph. That's not me. I plot vengeance against people for wrongs infinitely less serious than premeditated murder, human trafficking, etc. When I first got to grad school I met a woman who always obeyed the speed limit to the letter. If the sign said "45" she went 45…or less. It was so aggravating that I felt compelled to share my frustration. When a church member falls short of my expectations, I may forgive him. But it sometimes requires condescension.

God, forgive us not for wanting to be like you, but for the times we want to be you. We do such a horrible job at it. We make others doubt how loving you really are. I can embrace my own doubts—the doubts that come from you—but to make another person doubt because of our desire to play dress-up and wrench the scepter from your hand, that is horrible. Please, remind us:

We are your representatives. We are your people. We are your children. We are not you.

fifty-one || brave

You know that girl who had cancer, Julia? I found out that she decided to stay in school and to join the gymnastics team. The team traveled and she ended up speaking at another high school. She told them that they should trust in God. She told them her story. She told them that no one deserves cancer and that even though you don't have any control over it, you can control how you deal with it. You can either get angry at God and be bitter, or you can choose to remember that God still loves you.

I wanted to cry. I don't know how someone like her can say those words. I want to be angry at God for her, but how can I if she's not? She was just 16 when she found out she had cancer. How can she handle it so bravely? She's braver than I. Maybe she sees something I missed.

fifty-two || catching carmen

You may think that God found Adam and Eve, but that's not true. The people who limped out from behind the bushes were not the same people he had only recently eaten and played and done all sort of things with. Those people had changed. They were gone.

God called out for his children.

And God has been relentlessly searching the gardens of this world for his first children ever since that day. All through Exodus and Leviticus are littered these laws and requirements about ways people can become "clean" and "holy." Most Christians just skim past them on their way to the stories of Joshua and David. But those are beautiful and passionate passages of God saying, "Hey, I'm looking for people who will love like my first children did. This is what they look like. Are they any among you like them?" The requirements always boiled down to two at the end of the day: loving God and loving each other.

The search continued, and time after time the people who professed to be like God's first children hid from him. Jonah ran the other way and Joab looked the other way while David couldn't stay away. It was clear more drastic measures were needed.

God came down himself. Previously, he had said that his eyes roamed the earth, looking for people who were upright. But now he had eyes on the earth, enfleshed and touchable. Now he would look for his children in person. So the Christ lived among us like he once did at the beginning, calling people to come out of hiding and to follow him. He said, "I am what is true. I am the one who gave you life. I am the way back to the Father, back to your garden!" Many followed him, but some did not. So he told them, "When I am lifted up from the earth, I will draw all people to myself." He was lifted above the earth on a cross, so that all those still in hiding might see the depth of God's love; so that they might not be afraid to come out and embrace their God-friend. God came not just to find people, but to be found by them.

God didn't drag Adam and Eve from their hiding spot, scorning them for daring to think that they could bring sin into the world and then take no responsibility for it. God simply called out, asking them where they were. It's not that God didn't know where they were or anything. Adam and Eve thought they were hiding in the familiar setting of their garden, but God knew they were lost. Their sin hid his face from them, but they could still hear his voice. "Do you know where you are now, Adam?" he asked.

It's not God who is lost. God stands in the middle of his garden where he has always stood. It's me who has run away. And when I dare to shake my fist at God and ask, "Where were you when this happened?" he simply replies: "Right where you left me." And when I say, "Where is God when it hurts?" I must see that I am hiding among the thorns. And when I say, "This is good; it must be God!" it is only because I recognize that I am still hiding in his garden.

And he said, "I have come to find and rescue those who became lost."

fifty-three || thank you, jane austen

God is somewhat like Colonel Brandon. You know, an *ancient* at 35, humorless but persistent (the worst combination). He's faithful, too, but the kind of faithfulness that tempts transgression. We're flirting with the guys our age, chatting about who will inherit what and where we're all going in life. But Brandon is already beyond that. It doesn't mean anything to him. Plus, he's got history—a *lot* of history. He's been damaged (doesn't that explain it all?).

Enter John Willoughby. Dashing and charming, he's become the archetype for what all women love and fear. But he is present in a way that Colonel Brandon isn't—he's more in the moment, moving with and in and through the lives of people. When Brandon walks into a room, it's like time stops, like life is interrupted while he pauses to find a way to communicate with these people "below."

But it's kind of how some of us view Christianity. Of course we all know Colonel Brandon is the smarter match just as we know that we ought to turn the other cheek, not get drunk, and those sorts of things. But sometimes Christianity seems too solemn and weighty to handle life at full-speed. It seems like it will all be relevant tomorrow when I'm older, but not today. I find that I can really relate to it on the broad level—that I am innately evil and need help. But when it comes down to living with it in the day to day, it just doesn't get me. I can agree that the world is sinful and evil and that some people are going to hell. But it's harder to swallow when you ask me to believe those things about my friends.

The dear saints are right when they admonish us not to be "of the world," but sometimes I could swear they say it with a tinge of jealousy. Being a Christian is like having to take a vow of celibacy. At some point it's natural to wonder what it'd be like to have a family outside those walls. I mean that other-than-God stuff can be so much more exciting. Dashing and charming, like a Willoughby who rides gaily up to our front door with all the news of the world.

There's nothing wrong with "exciting," of course. We have no idea how the Bible characters got on having fun. But just because it's not mentioned doesn't mean they didn't toss a ball around or kick back with a couple of controllers and a video game. Maybe Abraham was a Sudoku nut. Who knows. But there seems to be this idea that if it's exciting and it's not a church event it's probably wrong. Bowling? Wrong atmosphere. Paintball? We don't want to be shooting people, now do we?

Just listen to the stories of some new Christians or from people who were committed non-Christians. They say things like, "I was having fun out there in the world...but I was living wholly for myself" in as solemn a voice as possible. But it's hard to miss the implication: you became selfless and no longer get any enjoyment out of life. It's either Colonel Brandon (boo) or John Willoughby (yay).

Why?

But God shouldn't be so easily typecast. We shouldn't see him as some celestial grandfather who cares enough only to dote on us with his warnings about staying away from those new "contraptions" such as radios and televisions because they're just evil and everyone knows it. Sometimes we think he was more relevant in an age of animal sacrifices and when people needed the gods to provide rain for their crops.

God doesn't have to be that guy.

The picture of God on earth is so different. He ate at the religious leaders' table and then talked with a blind man about faith and things. He went with all the people to Jerusalem on all the holidays but also took time sit on a Galilean hillside and tell people about what it means to be a good neighbor. Jesus was among the people. He wasn't some religious fanatic throwing rocks in the water. He was real and alive, surrounded by brambles and desert. But we try to protect him from the world by not taking him outside of church. That's where so many of us visit him, and that's where we leave him. Or maybe we're just embarrassed to introduce him to our non-church friends. If only he were more like Willoughby, then we could make him seem more like us.

Who is Jesus? If we could pick one character in all of the stories we've heard, who would he be most like? Oscar the Grouch? Superman? Mister Rodgers? Why do you think of him like you do?

Maybe he's not who we thought he was.

Maybe he's more.

fifty-four || in the beginning was the end

In the beginning God created with a single word. But in that word all his imagination burst forth into the dimensions of the universe. The word used for "create" is *bara*, which is only ever used in connection with God. God creates differently than we create. But he, like us, only creates things related to himself. And he, like us, creates things with a parent's hopes and fears.

Yet God saw the earth, waiting for his word. Darkness crawled over the silent pile of atoms that God had imagined. This world stood as an unpainted corner of his canvas. It was empty and formless, but it had such amazing potential. It had a deep, ancient history that it was as yet unaware of. God's Spirit hovered patiently just above the surface, waiting for the moment God would speak and bring life and beauty out of nothingness.

And God said, "Let there be light." And there was light, and it was the light of all people.

There was only darkness, but somehow God brought light out of it and pushed the darkness away. In an instant everything had changed. One moment, darkness, but in the next instant, light. The Spirit that waited so tirelessly to play his part plunged into this new world, so fresh with possibility. Now there was light, now there was room for him to work in amazing ways. And God saw that this light was good.

And God said, "There will be no more night…for the Lord God will give them light." And an angel watching from high heaven yelled out to the on-looking universe: "Look! God now dwells with his people and they shall never be separated. God has finished his masterpiece at last."

And his children shall say, "'In the beginning' was the end and the end was only the beginning."

God Is Love

Epilogue || Descartes

Descartes didn't actually say, "I doubt, therefore I think, therefore I am," though people think that he did. But doubts played an important role in his philosophy. Indeed, he came to believe in whatever was left standing after he raked his life over with doubt. What remained was what he was certain of, what he could count on.

He said: "Archimedes used to demand just one firm and immovable point in order to shift the entire earth; so I too can hope for great things if I manage to find just one thing, however slight, that is certain and unshakable."

That "one thing" he found was his certainty of his own existence. Even if God was playing tricks on him, even if everything we see is an illusion, he was there and that was enough. His ability to question, to second-guess and wonder "what if," confirmed, at the very least, that "he" (whatever that meant) existed.

That's the role doubt plays: it deconstructs our edifices and forces us to reexamine what beliefs are solid and reliable. How many times have you ever looked back and said, "Why did I ever believe that?" This isn't really an abstract, esoteric idea. Public buildings are inspected regularly to check for defects. Wood rots. Mortar crumbles. Steel rusts. There is nothing we humans can build that doesn't eventually become weak and fall over. It's not different when it comes to our ideas. We have to periodically check ourselves and make sure the foundations for our beliefs are solid.

Let doubt in and don't hold back. Start with the small things, but don't be afraid to question the big things, too. It's okay to be afraid. Chances are you'll wind up right back where you started. But you will be stronger. You will find fresh faith alongside with new doubts. Rediscover the one thing that is "certain and unshakeable" and rebuild from there.

And then do it again.

Keep rebuilding your house throughout your life and one day, when you step back, you will notice that you're part of a neighborhood with streets of gold.

Index of Scriptures

So Loved	Matthew 19:29
	Mark 10:30
	John 5
I Doubt	Exodus 32
	Revelation 22:2
Questions	Job 30:20-21
	Jeremiah 12:1-2
	Ecclesiastes 3:19
E8	Ecclesiastes 8:10-18
	(paraphrased)
Soon*	Psalm 90:4
	2 Peter 3:9
	Luke 18:1-8
	Rev. 6:9-11
Therefore I Think	2 Kings 6:15-17
Promises, Promises	Isaiah 43:1, 4
When Angels Attack	Genesis 32:22-32
Woodstock	Joshua 5:13-14

Dreams	Daniel 7
Wept	John 11:35
Thief	Revelation 16:15 Matthew 24:33, 36
Ready (Or Not)	Matthew 24:22 Matthew 24:11
Disguised	Exodus 19
Therefore I AM	Matthew 27:46 Matthew 27:54 John 8:58 John 20:28
Jealousy	Song of Solomon 8:6
Dirge	Matthew 11:17
Snakes	Exodus 8:19
DH905569	Genesis 32:28
Empty	Ephesians 4:30
Home	Matthew 25:14-30 Revelation 14:6, 7 Isaiah 25:9, 8
Fifteen Years	Isaiah 38, 39

Vicar	Genesis 50
Catching Carmen	Genesis 3:8 Deuteronomy 6:5 Leviticus 19:8 2 Chronicles 16:9 Psalm 33:18 John 14:6 John 12:32 Isaiah 59:2 Luke 19:10
In the Beginning...	Genesis 1:1 John 1:4 Revelation 22:5 Revelation 21:3

Eulogies

It's a strange thing when you get to this page. It's definitely not the most interesting thing to read. You probably don't know who these people are and, frankly, you have little reason to hope to meet them.

But that's not to say they're in any way unremarkable. I only mean that their contributions aren't on a global scale. They have no recipe for world peace or how to resolve the massive theological rows that have existed for centuries. Rather, they are friends. And friends whose own gifts can help you use yours. It's easy to find people you have things in common with. But finding people who can help you reach your goals is much deeper.

So permit me to eulogize them in a few lines because, as I said, you probably won't get to meet them.

Without Kayla McAuliffe this book never would have gotten off of the ground. She's not exactly the "rah rah" cheerleading type. (Actually, she's pretty much the opposite.) But she is an awesome editor. Her strange taste for low budget BBC shows is proof of this. When I was reviewing her changes, there were random references in the margin to this book or that T.V. show. So if any out-of-place literary references show up in this book, you'll know who to blame. Even though she's destined to be a school counselor, I'd really love to see her be an editor somewhere, so someone out there please give her a job.

Christina Bratlund did her best to keep me orthodox. Despite her desire to keep me from being burned at the stake, I am sure there are some parts of this book she's going to wince at. (I'm sorry, Christina.) Her advice was always well-reasoned and I'm sure this is owed to the fact that she is among the first wave of my peers to get their PhD. I am proud of her, even though I have very little idea what speech pathology is.

This brings us to Jason Vanderlaan. Jason is crazy creative in a silent, self-contained way. He's not the sort that would violently assault a canvas with paint after a break-up. He's the sort who eviscerates you in poetry in such a subtle way that you actually like the poem without realizing it's about you. He's a prolific writer and a trusted friend to a lot of people. Virtually every creative decision I make has his fingerprints on it. He's put up with me with great grace, yet he has vented a few heavy *sighs* at my antics. While Kayla would justly chasten me for my use of ambigious pronouns, Jason softened it a bit and only cautioned me about my "slightly" ambigious pronouns. More than all this, he's been my twin in many respects. We should have been born brothers and I have schemed through the years about how to become related in some way or the other. I have always been confident that I would get married before him, though I am no longer willing to put money on it. I don't want to be robbed of my right hand, but I've come to terms with it at last. Besides, I have so many wonderful things to say at his reception...

Of course I'd like to thank my family and all the various influences that have unknowingly imprinted themselves in this book. We are all only sub-creators, owing our ideas in large part to others and, ultimately, to our God.

Of him it has been said: "In Him I live, and move, and have my existence."

In Him I doubt.

In Him I trust.

-

For more books from
Balm and Blade Publishing,
including Unspoken Confessions
and Fire by T. Jason Vanderlaan,
or for the latest news and updates,

please visit:
balmandblade.com

or join us on either
Facebook or Twitter.

www.ingramcontent.com/pod-product-compliance
Lightning Source LLC
Chambersburg PA
CBHW032134040426
42449CB00005B/244